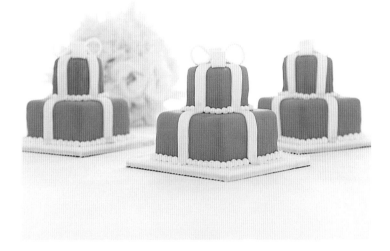

simple stunn

ng weddings

DESIGNING AND CREATING YOUR PERFECT CELEBRATION

Karen Bussen

Photographs by
Ellen Silverman

STEWART, TABORI & CHANG • NEW YORK

FOR MY SISTER SARA

Text copyright © 2004 Karen Bussen
Photographs on pages 4–5, 10, 14, 18, 19,
22, 23, 32, and 47 by Brad Paris

All other photographs
copyright © 2004 Ellen Silverman

Published in 2004 by
Stewart, Tabori & Chang
115 West 18th Street
New York, NY 10011
www.abramsbooks.com

Canadian Distribution:
Canadian Manda Group
One Atlantic Avenue, Suite 105
Toronto, Ontario M6K 3E7
Canada

Library of Congress Cataloging-in-
Publication Data

Bussen, Karen.
  Simple stunning weddings / by Karen
Bussen ; photographs by Ellen Silverman.
    p. cm.
  ISBN 1-58479-365-1
1. Weddings—Planning. 2. Simplicity. I.
Title.
  HQ745.B88 2004
  395.2'2—dc22   2004000513

Designed by Susi Oberhelman

The text of this book was composed in
Helvetica Neue and New Caledonia

Printed in China

10 9 8 7 6 5 4 3 2

Stewart, Tabori & Chang is a subsidiary of
LA MARTINIÈRE GROUPE

contents

invitation to SIMPLICITY

"Making the simple

complicated is commonplace;

Making the complicated

simple, awesomely simple,

that's creativity."

Charles Mingus

Infuse your celebration with simple, meaningful details. A small book of love poems paired with a keepsake bookmark makes a wonderful gift for your guests or your wedding party. Add a handwritten note inside for a special touch.

The journey toward your wedding day likely started with one simple word—"Yes." If only your wedding celebration could be so easy! But, unlike the brides and grooms of ancient times whose thumbs or hands were simply tied together with a leather, lace or piece of fabric (thereby, "tying the knot"), you have much more to think about when it comes to saying "I do" in a way that is personal, lovely, and meaningful.

I've met so many brides and grooms who feel overwhelmed by the enormity of creating what is often the most important party of their lives. They want their dream day to be infused with the spirit and magic of their love and their personalities, but aren't sure how to make it happen. When I meet with couples to discuss their wedding design, the looming question is, "How are we going to pull it all together?" This is generally followed by the lament, "We had no idea how many decisions there are to make." When I tell them not to worry, that we'll start with the setting, look at their vision for the day, and then begin to pare down our choices, they immediately relax—a little bit.

You may have a general idea of the way you want your special day to feel, and perhaps you know a few of the elements you want to include, such as a particular color or flower, but the many details that need to be attended to, and the task of managing your florist, band, caterer, photographer, wedding party, and guests can be confusing and stressful. Family pressures, design and etiquette decisions, priorities—it's a delicate balance you must achieve to avoid conflict and miscommunications along the way. Making things more difficult, there are really no hard and fast formulas for today's couples to follow. There are so many possibilities and such a variety of options for everything from caterers to candles that it can all seem truly daunting.

imiting the number of types of flowers in your bouquets and centerpieces is both elegant and economical. A small posy of perfect, striking blossoms, such as these miniature mango-hued calla lilies, makes a dramatic and colorful statement.

This book is designed to help you create your perfect wedding mood, as simply as possible. My goal is to share basic information about party design principles, and illustrate them through twelve common wedding settings. This will help you identify and refine your vision for your wedding, and will prepare you to discuss it with your loved ones and your chosen vendors in a clear, concise way.

Equally important, I aim to inspire you visually (with the help of Ellen Silverman's amazing photographs) to take advantage of the power and beauty of a simple approach when it comes to your own wedding. I've designed each wedding in this book to demonstrate practical, beautiful ways to keep your celebration both simple and stunning. I hope you'll pull ideas from as many of the chapters as appeal to you, to personalize and enhance your own chosen setting.

what is simple?

Simplicity, to me, is an aesthetic that is both classic and contemporary, elegant and unfussy. It begins with a clear vision of your intended mood or ambiance, and defines itself in direct relation to its environment.

A simple wedding can be inexpensive or extremely luxurious, depending upon the materials, setting, food, and other elements you choose. My simple approach to design is less about budget than about planning details—color, flowers, menu—to create a powerful mood, whether your wedding is casual or formal. It is worth noting, however, that a simple wedding design will almost always be less wasteful (and more stylish) than one that is over-the-top. This book will help you to discover and articulate the mood of your wedding with confidence and common sense, beginning from where I feel it all starts: your location.

10 simple stunning truths

Keep these basic ideas in mind when making decisions about your wedding design.

1. **Simple is not the same as cheap.** A simple wedding design stems from a clear vision which is in harmony with the chosen setting. Your preferences for linens, flowers, even menu items, as well as your location and the size of your party, will determine your costs. A wedding feast for 50 guests in a 5-star restaurant is one of the simplest celebrations you can choose. However, fine restaurants are not inexpensive, and many charge à premium for renting private rooms or the entire space.

2. **Simple is not necessarily minimal.** A simple design uses restraints to create a more powerful effect; however, there are times when a single element, such as one type of flower, can be multiplied beautifully to express what I consider an "extravagance of simplicity." Imagine one 32-foot long table with a single cotton tablecloth sewn to full length. Picture one flower—a poppy—repeated 100 times in narrow glass vases placed down the center of the table. It's easy to see that this design is highly streamlined, but also abundant in its own way. Here, simplicity means limiting *types* of materials, colors, etc., to achieve a stronger visual effect. Whether you'll need a lot or a little of your chosen

materials will depend on your setting, the size of your party, your preferences, and your budget.

3. **Simple stunning weddings** are focused and in harmony with your sensibility and your environment. Take the time to think about and discuss with each other the type of party you want. Brainstorm first, and make a list of your wedding priorities. Then choose your setting with care and design your party to suit your setting.

4. **Great weddings are comfortable parties.** Never make a design choice in favor of "the look" if it will compromise your guests' ability to enjoy your party. Let's say you love the idea of long tables in your reception space. But the space is narrow, and arranging the tables this way would make it harder for waiters to serve your guests food and drinks. The tables may look gorgeous, but if servers will have to resort to bumping into the guests' chairs, and reaching around one guest to get to another, your family and friends (and your service staff) will be uncomfortable. If long tables are a must for you, you should choose a space that can comfortably accommodate your party.

5. **A stunning wedding is as simple as 1-2-3.** This means that as many elements as possible are limited to no more than three choices. Color is the most important example. For the most powerful impact, focus on a maximum of three colors in each area you're designing. When selecting linens, flow-ers, even printed materials, using tones of just reds and pinks set against a white background will create a more striking, harmonious aesthetic than, say, a room filled with a riot of yellows, pinks, oranges, purples, blues, and greens. It also makes your design selection process a lot more streamlined, as you will automatically rule out colors which are not a part of your plan. You can certainly use different colors in your ceremony than at your reception, but within any one space, try to narrow your choices. For flow-ers I recommend no more than three types in each arrangement. Apply 1-2-3 principle to as many elements as possible and you will be surprised at the stunning effect.

6. **Simple stunning weddings are never trendy.** Simple design, by its very nature, is both classic and contemporary, with an emphasis on well-chosen details, not the latest fads. For example, a wedding table dressed with good, crisp white linen will always be in style. Accented with unfussy bouquets of just one type of seasonal blossom, it is both timeless and chic.

dramatic flowers and vases can stand alone. When you feature unusual flowers and strong shapes, just two or three blossoms are enough, especially when the form is repeated. We paired geometric apple-green resin vases with "pin cushion" protea and gloriosa lilies in tangerine for this modern summer wedding.

7. **Weddings should have a unifying theme.** Whether it's a color or a culinary focus, choosing a central theme that works in your setting guarantees a more harmonious mood for your celebration. A Zen-style wedding might feature an invitation on beautifully folded rice paper, a sake and sushi hour instead of the usual hors d'oeuvres, floating orchids on the tables, and party favors of Asian candies or green tea. When all design choices fall into line with an overall theme, from fonts to foods, the result is not only more appealing, it also simplifies the planning process.

Centerpieces don't have to be overflowing. Floating flowers and candles are both romantic and easy on the budget, as you need only a few of each. For contemporary settings, choose orchids, daisies, dahlias, or sunflowers. In more classical surroundings, try gardenias, peonies, or garden roses.

8. **Couples should know their design priorities.** There is more than one way to decorate any setting: the possibilities can seem endless. Make lists of the things that are most important to you. Flowers? Music? Food? Each couple feels differently about which details are more crucial. Write down your priorities and then stick to them every step of the way.

Discuss your priorities with all vendors at your first meeting to make sure you understand each other (and if you don't, find another vendor!). Use the advantages your location has to offer rather than trying to make it something it isn't. If you're inflexible about your setting, you might need to prepare for complications. A beach wedding, for example, suggests a certain set of party options, generally somewhat casual. If you're the bride and groom who want a formal ten-course surfside feast, it can be done, but you'll have to be ready to deal with a myriad of details to make it happen.

9. **Simplicity is well-planned.** Knowing your priorities is the key to maintaining your design focus and your sanity, but you'll also want to be open to new possibilities along the way. Of course, if your invitations have already been printed or custom linens already sewn, this flexibility might no longer be possible. If you evaluate your priorities thoroughly from the start, you'll likely avoid any major changes. Look at any new idea in relation to your overall theme, and decide whether the change will adversely affect the whole event, or add something wonderful.

10. **Simpler is better.** Take the time to apply simple stunning principles. Focus your budget, your preferences, and your approach on smart details and gracious warmth rather than pomp and prestige, and you'll be rewarded with a stunningly beautiful, headache-free wedding day. The result is worth the effort: On your golden anniversary, I guarantee you'll treasure the memory of your festive, romantic day, and you'll toast each other's good sense and great style.

how to
use this book

If you already know where you'll be celebrating, you'll find this book filled with hundreds of simple, beautiful inspirations for your big day. In addition, an "Inspiration Box" for each location offers even more ideas.

The most important choice you'll make about your wedding celebration is where it will take place. All other details—the menu, the wedding dress, the invitation, the flowers, and all the other choices you must make—will flow from your decision to be married in a particular setting.

If you haven't yet chosen your location, this book may help you figure out what is best for your special day by describing the advantages and challenges of twelve of the most common wedding situations. Each chapter focuses on one special venue—Beach, Restaurant, Hotel—and provides a "simplicity meter," a quick indicator of what you might be getting yourself into in terms of logistics, décor, and personalization. Then there's plenty of inside information on what you need to know, places you might want to splurge, ways to keep it simple and stunning, and what *not* to attempt on your own.

Once you've narrowed it down to a few choices, you can use the facts and photos in the book as a reference point for discussions with family, florists, and everyone else who will have a hand in helping you design and plan your wedding. Basic design techniques such as color and clustering will help you to be confident and in control of your vision. I've also included chapters about the ceremony, and an overview of budget issues, with lots of helpful hints for keeping wedding finances as uncomplicated as possible.

I've tried to focus on ideas and materials that are readily available to most couples, via the Internet or mail order, and on linens and other décor that can be easily substituted if necessary. This is a design book for real weddings, and although the weddings encompass a range of budgets, I've avoided concepts that are just fantastical or unable to be reproduced. You should be able to use this book as a reference when talking to your vendors, and they should be able to suggest alternatives when something you want is unavailable.

Here are some terms of the trade that may be unfamiliar to you. "Vendors," or "service provider" means florists, caterers, musicians, photographers, videographers, printers, delivery people, attire rental companies, tent professionals—in short, anyone who will contribute goods or services to your wedding celebration.

"Venue" means your ceremony or reception location.

"Destination" or "weekend-getaway" weddings are terms for celebrations that are held at some distance from the bride's or groom's home-town, usually a tourist-friendly location or resort area, offering great opportunities for additional wedding-related activities.

Other terms, such as "clustering" and "flow," are discussed in the next chapter.

Start by thumbing through these pages. Let your imagination guide you. Once you've chosen your wedding location, begin to focus on the design principles of simplicity and beauty. Refer back to Chapter One! Use as many of the tips and ideas as apply and appeal to you, staying focused on your color palette and your key elements. Don't obsess over details—trust your instincts instead and remember, the most memorable weddings overflow with an abundance of grace, meaning, style, and substance.

Here's to your simple stunning wedding!

KAREN BUSSEN

bold color combinations work well in simple, modern spaces. You can tailor your presentation by wrapping simple glass or plastic vases with ribbon to match your colors. All you need is a roll of ribbon, a pair of scissors, and a can of spray adhesive from the craft store.

stunningly SIMPLE

Your wedding celebration, with all the planning, family politics, stress, and finances involved, is already complicated enough. Sometimes the number of options and decisions can become overwhelming and frustrating. But there are lots of ways to pare down and simplify your wedding while still creating a stunning atmosphere filled with meaningful, unique touches. As you read the rest of the book, come back to this chapter to help keep you focused.

his table setting is all about shape and color. Square pillar and votive candles echo the geometry of the glassware, charger plates, and sleek chair covers. A few sprigs of ilex berry branches add a soft, natural element to this very modern look.

● **Let your surroundings inspire every aspect of your wedding.** Resist clichés or kitschy concepts and honor the space you've chosen with well-placed, timeless details. If you're at the beach, let the sea inspire your party. If you're in a traditional space, include classical details and a bit more formality. If your space is filled with modern glass and metal, use these elements

colorful lanterns add a whimsical touch to the soaring scale of a tent ceiling. Check stores or the Internet to find the many types of inexpensive lanterns available (above). Unusual can be delightful. For a buffet-style cocktail hour, we decorated food stations with geometric clusters of prickly pear cactus, okra, and peppers, which (if undamaged) can be reused or donated to charity (opposite).

and a minimal approach in your centerpieces and invitations.

- **Consider the flow of your celebration.** As you are choosing your location and throughout your planning process, keep in mind how your guests will transition from one space to another during your wedding. Provide for clear well-lit paths and rain plans, and make arrangements for any guests who might have mobility issues. Plan for necessary space transformations, such as turning your ceremony space into your dining room, so that guests won't be disturbed during the party. And make sure there are adequate parking facilities, elevators, and emergency exits. Your party flow can also be affected by other celebrations taking place at your location. Find out in advance if there will be other events on your wedding day. If so, discuss timing, staffing, service—and even noise—issues with your venue representative.

- **Create a color story for each space.** Remember the simple stunning principle of limiting each room to a maximum of three colors in your design wherever possible. But do alter your color scheme for various spaces or parts of the celebration. This gives your guests a visual treat, and keeps the party exciting.

- **Do your homework.** Use the Internet, local chambers of commerce, and the advice of friends, colleagues, and family to help you make sound choices for locations, vendors, even timelines.

- **Ask lots of questions in advance, if possible.** Don't be intimidated—you've probably never planned a party this big before. You need information—and lots of it. Reputable vendors will be happy to provide you with everything you need to know.

- **Get it in writing.** Have a detailed written contract or agreement with every location, and service provider you use, and keep them organized. Insist on receipts for deposits and vendor insurance certificates wherever appropriate.

- **Focus your design budget.** Decide what is most important to you. If your space is already highly decorated, you won't need much. If you absolutely must be married next to the pond at your parents' home, you'll need a tent. If you're both musicians, you might want an orchestra for dancing at dinner. The more you know your priorities, and stick with them, the better you'll be able to spend where it counts and pare down where it doesn't.

- **Use your vendors as resources.** People in the industry are in the know. Photographers can recommend great florists, and caterers know of good rental companies. Take advantage of their expertise.

- **Think out of the box.** A single floating flower surrounded by a ring of glowing votives can be a more elegant centerpiece than a humongous candelabra arrangement. Ten perfect calla lilies in a simple vase can be as striking as fifty or a hundred, if artfully arranged. Use fruits, vegetable, plants, even candles as your centerpieces, or line your table with inexpensive vases, each holding just one flower.

Laurel Gray

- **Have a theme.** Your celebration can be centered on a color, an element of nature, a place, a poem, or an attitude. Just make sure your theme is in harmony with the location you've chosen, then layer your party with details that relate to the theme. Use it in your centerpieces, printed materials, cake, menu, and party favors.

- **Choose people you like to work with.** Don't choose a vendor just because he or she is "the best" or "the cheapest." Your wedding is exactly that—yours—and you must be comfortable and happy with the people who are helping you make it happen. Interview several vendors for each key element of your celebration. Check references and then follow your instincts. Request tastings and samples wherever possible so you will feel confident you've made the right choice.

- **Set limits.** Apply the simple stunning principle of limiting types of flowers, types of cuisines, and types of materials. There is power in making a design choice and following through with it. Mix no more than three kinds of flowers in one container, and stick to glass, metal, or ceramic vases—not all three. Don't try to do Moroccan, Zen, and Tuscan all in the same room. Pick one and take it all the way!

- **Infuse your celebration with meaning.** Write a quote on your cake, or ask your parents to write a poem or read a special passage at the wedding. Include a personal note in your ceremony program. Display pictures of you and your family at the reception. Remember those who

a silver tray from the flea market, with white pillar and votive candles nestled on a bed of rose petals, makes a great (and less expensive) centerpiece (above). Materials matter. Look to your location for inspiration. For this contemporary loft wedding, we paired a polished aluminum vase and tea light holder with vivid yellow calla lilies (opposite).

a luxury of simplicity. For this wedding, we hand-lettered square red votive candles with each guest's name and table number. The candles were alphabetically arranged on shelves in a special tent. Imagine 300 guests walking to their tables with flickering lights!

can't be with you. Involve your guests in your ceremony with candle-lighting ceremonies. Use your natural surroundings—trees, gardens, architecture—as symbols of your union, incorporating them into your ceremony and your party.

- **Don't overdecorate your ceremony.** Keep it simple and reverential, using music, readings, and your wedding party to bring spirit and beauty to this special moment. Carry small posies or single-stems instead of unwieldy, cascading bouquets. Avoid view-blocking aisle décor. Instead, decorate chairs or pews with a ribbon-tied blossom or a small swag.

- **Cluster your design elements.** Grouping coordinated items, such as vases, lanterns and candles, provides a powerful punch. If you can't afford or don't want large centerpieces, try clustering smaller vases together with just a single bloom or a small bouquet of flowers in each. The impact lies in the interesting arrangement of these shapes, lines and colors. The same principle applies to other elements as well. If your venue has two couches and few ottomans or armchairs, arrange them all together in one corner or at the edge of the dance floor to create a lounge-like area, rather than dispersing them throughout. Guests will want to gather there. If you have 25 paper lanterns, cluster them over the entrance or above the dance floor rather than spreading them out across the whole ceiling. Their colors and shapes will read more powerfully in a group than when dispersed over a larger space.

- **Don't do everything yourself.** Decide what you want to do, but don't take up a new occupation, wiring your own floral bouquets or baking multitiered fondant cakes on the eve of your wedding, no matter how easy that magazine made it look. There are certain tasks which should be left to the pros, or at least to the unengaged. Be realistic, enlist the help of talented, dependable friends wherever possible, and add your own handiwork where it will be noticed, appreciated, and minimally stressful.

- **Focus your budget.** Simplify your bar, offering just beer, wine, and soft drinks. Or spend more on cocktail hour, and keep your dinner menu streamlined. Hire a deejay instead of a big band. Choose a silk or other pretty tablecloth and accent it with simple candles instead of large floral centerpieces.

- **Pay attention to lighting.** I consider lighting to be one of the most crucial elements in creating atmosphere. Inquire about adjustable light levels at your venue and find out whether spotlights and accent lights are available for your centerpieces and any architectural elements. Visit your space at the time of day you will be hosting your wedding to be sure you're happy with the lighting levels. Supplement with candles where permitted and, if necessary or desired, inquire about a professional lighting designer.

- **Make quality choices.** Use linen napkins. Host a cocktail party, but offer the finest foods and wines. Highlight one single, perfect rare orchid

for your centerpieces, rather than a jumble of less expensive flowers. Choose vendors who provide excellent products and personal service, even if they're a bit more expensive—you do get what you pay for, and you and your guests will notice the difference.

- **Check the excess.** Do you really need those extra pedestals and flowers at the entrance? Must you arrive in a white SUV limousine, or could you just ask a family member to drive you? Are you sure you need the caviar bar, the sushi chefs *and* the carving station—for cocktails? Decide where you'll gain the most "bang for your buck," and then make choices to surprise and delight your guests, not overwhelm them.
- **Give meaningful gifts to your guests.** Whether it's a living tree or plant, a keepsake bud vase from your centerpieces, or a donation to your favorite charity, reuse, recycle, and remember: it's the thought that counts.
- **Never skimp on service.** A well cared-for guest is a happy guest. Make sure you'll have enough waiters for the style of service you've chosen. Have coat-check facilities and parking attendants available wherever appropriate. Insist that someone be responsible for checking the bathrooms throughout your celebration, and make sure you know who's in charge in case there's a problem. Think about your guests' comfort and you'll be the best hosts ever.
- **Don't forget about safety.** Look at your locations to insure your guests' comfort and security.

Are hand railings, stairways, and paths secure and well-lit? Are parking facilities attended? Will there be a security staff member on site in case of a problem during your wedding? I strongly advise making advance arrangements to transport any guests who've done a bit too much celebrating. Call a local shuttle bus or taxi service or enlist the help of your caterer or venue to find a reputable provider for this important service.

- **Book as early as possible.** Great locations, vendors, even officiants book up quickly. Once you've set your date, make arrangements as soon as possible. If you're planning in the short-term, take it step by step and try to be flexible.
- **Don't forget to ask for extras.** Extra rooms, discounts, more time for setup, more hors d'oeuvres. You know what they say about the squeaky wheel!
- **Think about your wedding memories.** If you want to attend your cocktail hour, take your photographs before the ceremony. If you'd rather not see each other before the ceremony, limit the number of after-ceremony portraits so you won't miss the reception.

this romantic centerpiece is made of just ten stems of pale blue hydrangea, one for each of the small julep cups (used as guest favors), and five stems for the taller central vase. Rented romantic glassware and a blue floral tablecloth with a pale blue satin bow for each napkin complete the look.

- **Consider hiring a professional videographer.** If you choose one with an unobtrusive approach, they'll capture parts of the party you might miss, and document your ceremony without disturbing you or your guests. I guarantee you'll love seeing this footage later.

- **Create a contact list.** Organize this list by category: photographer, caterer, band, florist, etc., and Email or fax it to each of your vendors and your wedding day coordinator or banquet manager. This way if there's any problem, concern or question, everyone knows whom to contact.

- **Put someone else in charge.** On the day of your wedding, neither the bride nor the groom should be running the show or troubleshooting. If you don't have a wedding planner, appoint a member of your wedding party or a trusted family member or friend to be the liaison between your venue and vendors. Have a meeting with this person in advance and go over all contact information and timelines to make sure your wishes are honored and everything comes off without a hitch. I've seen weddings where the bride is running around trying to put out fires—don't let this be you!

- **Take an extra day to rest before the honeymoon.** This way, you can have a farewell brunch with your guests, take a nap, and finish packing before your trip. I've seen a lot of brides and grooms too exhausted to truly enjoy this wonderful part of their new life together.

- **Plan in advance.** Discuss rain alternatives for your outdoor ceremony. Introduce your vendors to each other prior to the wedding day. Meet your on-site catering or banquet staff beforehand to make a connection. Don't wait till the last minute to find out how much air-conditioning for your tents or calligraphy for the place cards will cost. The more organized you are up-front, the better.

- **Relax, no matter what, and enjoy your big day.** Rain is good luck at weddings and no one but you (and maybe your mom) will notice that fake flower arrangement the staff forgot to remove, or that ugly smudge on the wall. It just doesn't matter! You've planned and prepared the best you can—now you should be "in the moment," blissfully focused on the fact that you're beginning a wonderful, exciting new life together on this very special day!

antique lace gives a vintage touch to these cloudlike bouquets of feathery white nerene (foreground) and soft ranunculus (background). Roses, tulips, or lisianthus would be just as lovely. As a special touch, the bride clasped a silver and crystal bracelet around each bouquet as a thank-you and keepsake for her attendants.

a simple BUDGET

Without a doubt, creating and sticking to a budget can be one of the most complicated, stressful, overwhelming, and difficult aspects of planning your wedding. Chances are you've never thought about how much it costs to rent 10,000 square feet of party space, or 100 oyster forks. Most likely, you don't know the going rate for a top-notch videographer or a good chef. And there are hundreds of these kinds of decisions to be made throughout the process of planning a wedding.

think out of the box. These plastic—yes, plastic!—cocktail glasses made perfect vases. A single stem of white hydrangea in each is impressive when the vases are grouped together, and less expensive than a larger mixed arrangement. Check stores that sell housewares, and look for great colors to match your party.

Many of the choices you make will affect your overall cost, from the location of your celebration, to the time of year, from the day of the week, the style of food and service you will provide, the size of your guest list and bridal party, to the music, flowers, linens, lighting, sound, printing, favors, welcome baskets, attire, and transportation. It may

seem like the list of items you must buy, rent, purchase, or guarantee goes on forever.

I have met many couples who didn't have a budget nailed down at the outset, or who didn't want to think about it. "We just have no idea," is a popular response to my initial questions about budget. For some couples the wedding is the first time they've had to discuss financial matters together. For others, there may be personal issues about money or family generosity that can create conflict and tension.

On the other hand, I recently received a call from a bride's father (before I ever even met the bride or groom!) who said very matter-of-factly, "I want to spend X dollars. Can you do everything for that amount?"

Neither one of these scenarios is ideal, but at least the latter, while less romantic, provided a helpful starting point for our discussions. Would my team be coordinating this wedding or just designing it? How large were the guest list and bridal party? Did his budget number include the ceremony or just the reception? Would the venue require lighting design? Linens? Who would be creating the invitations? The answers to these questions helped us establish a framework from which we could plan.

who's paying?

The first thing to think about is where the money will come from. Traditionally, the bride's family was responsible for the big day. That just isn't the

d on't overdecorate your cocktail tables (above). Votives or a small bud vase is enough. This couple chose to add personalized matchboxes, available on the Internet. Celebrate the beauty of each flower. This simple, but showy half-stem of a cymbidium orchid spray invites everyone's admiration (opposite).

case anymore. These days the finances to pay for a wedding come from many different sources. I've recently designed two large weddings which were funded by and mostly planned by the groom's family. Often, both families contribute, sometimes equally, sometimes each agreeing to pay for certain aspects or elements, such as the honeymoon, the band, or the food.

Of course, financial discussions with family (and with each other) can be a tender subject, especially because there can be a sense that whoever is funding the party has a degree of control or at least input over the decisions, from the guest list to color choices. And unless your family has hosted multiple weddings, there may not be a realistic sense of how much wedding services really cost or what is involved.

A growing number of my clients, especially those who are slightly older and more established (or just committed to saving up for a while), are paying for most of the celebration themselves. Another scenario is the couple who "make up the difference" for elements which are important to them. Recently one bride I was working with, when confronted with family-imposed budget cuts to her flower décor, decided that since orchids were a priority for her, she would pay the difference.

Consider your unique situation. Make a list of who will be contributing to the expenses and be sure to note if they've specified how they'd like their money to be used. Several of my clients and their families have opened joint "Wedding Fund" checking accounts to streamline the process. Others like to

divide the expenses and pay for them individually. Some pay for everything by check or money order, while others use a credit card, even for large amounts.

If your starting number is a very specific figure, you can consider yourself lucky. A finite budget helps limit the seemingly limitless options, details and "upgrades" which will present themselves throughout the process. On the other hand, if your budget is more flexible, you might have a greater comfort level, knowing that as unexpected issues come up there's a bit of room to adjust.

Either way, your next step is to create a list of priorities. Every couple has a few elements which are more important than others. For some, it's location—I designed a wedding for a New York City couple who had a special connection to a particular university. Not only had they met and fallen in love there as students, but both of their fathers were alumni of the college. Although it would have been much easier and more convenient for them to have hosted their 300-guest gathering in New York City at a hotel or loft space, there was no question in their minds that they would be married on campus. Their choice of location was certainly more expensive, as we had to construct tents and transport staff and refrigerated trucks full of flowers (and tables, and chairs, and kitchen equipment!) out of the city, but it was one of the most magical weddings I have ever been a part of. The feeling of connectedness between the bride's and groom's families, their circle of college friends, and the beautiful setting, all made it unforgettably special.

what matters most?

Whether you've got a firm number to work from or more flexibility, you should start by asking yourselves and each other questions about seasons, places, people, mood—the more questions you ask, the better, and the more specific they are, the better. Some of the answers may be obvious right away; others may take a bit of discussion. Sit down separately first, and make a list of your top three to five priorities, then review them together. This way, you'll know from the beginning what is most important to you and to your partner, and you'll have a good starting point for focusing your resources.

Magazines and books often advise allotting a specific percentage of your budget to this element of the wedding or that. I've just never found these formulas to work when I've tried to apply them to real weddings. The costs for bands, venues, and caterers really do vary widely, and individual preferences and choices will throw off any average

a tent wedding can be expensive, as every single element must be brought in for your celebration. Throughout the process, consider your priorities and look for ways to save. Streamline your choices, and ask for updated estimates as you finalize your choices for food, décor, rentals, and other details.

statistics. Of course, for most weddings food and beverage are a major expense, but even with those there is such a wide range of options.

Having said the above, if it helps you to have a general starting point for your budget planning, allow 50% for your location rental, food, and beverages. Taking your priorities into account, allot the other 50% for décor, attire, photography, stationery, and miscellaneous costs such as transportation.

where do you want to be?

Your chosen location will almost always be affected by the things you value and enjoy. For example, if being outdoors in the early autumn is a priority for you, you'll immediately begin to explore locations which offer this possibility. If fine wine and food are high on your list of priorities, you might be happier in a restaurant or vineyard than on a beach.

Once you have set your priorities and your location, you can do the research needed to determine the specific costs associated with hosting your wedding. If it's an elegant beach soirée you want, you might start looking for a private event facility or a fine hotel on the water. If you prefer a casual clambake, then a weekend home or a local public beach might work. You can use friends, the Internet, local publications, even the chamber of commerce to help you determine which place will fit in with your wishes and your budget.

this simple white place card was printed with a home computer, and accented with a pressed paper flower purchased from a local stationery store (above). Why not use glass cake stands or platters found in a flea market to hold colorful votives? Add just a few orchid blossoms for a budget-friendly, unique table decoration (opposite).

money matters

Your budget planning will depend upon your financial resources, family contributions, and other factors. Many couples start with an overall number and make adjustments and choices accordingly, tailoring the party to suit the budget. Others begin by establishing the size and style of the wedding they want, then calculating their expected costs. Either way, it's important to remember a few things when thinking about your finances.

Plants last longer, and can be less expensive than cut flowers. Here a mix of vintage-style silver urns with small topiaries makes an English-garden-style centerpiece. Use a single plant in the center of your tables, or cluster multiples and give them away as gifts to your guests. Check your local nursery for what's available in your wedding season.

First, every wedding budget is different. Statistics show the current national average cost for a wedding is just above $20,000, but couples are celebrating their marriages every day at every possible budget level. You must determine what will work for you and your families. Although your wedding is a momentous occasion, you don't want to begin your new lives together under the stress of debt or lost savings.

Second, the beauty of a wedding ultimately has nothing to do with how much money is spent. It's easy to lose sight of this fact with all of the information, products, and services available to brides and grooms today. But in the end creativity, thoughtfulness, and well-chosen details will add so much more to your celebration than giant candelabras. I promise.

everyone has a budget

Don't feel bad if you don't have a fortune to spend on your wedding. Every single couple I work with has a budget limit, some higher, some lower, and most of them feel it's not enough to do everything they want. The secret lies in remembering what is most important about your wedding day—being with family and friends, and celebrating your love! Repeat this to yourself as often as necessary to avoid succumbing to the contagious wedding ailment I call "detail derailment." I have seen reasonable brides and grooms morph into minutiae-obsessed party hosts as the big day approaches.

I once timed a conversation I had with a couple and their parents, who were debating which rented coffee cup was better looking. After seventeen minutes, I pointed out that both of the cups were white, one a little whiter than the other. Fortunately, everyone laughed, and as soon as I had made the observation that what was really crucial here was that the coffee should be good and hot, we all relaxed. In the effort to create a beautiful party, it's very easy to lose sight of what the day is all about. Don't let that happen to you, no matter what.

simple
budget advice

- **Begin with a starting number, or at least an acceptable range.** Don't avoid discussing money directly with each other, your families, and any prospective vendors or service providers. But do remember that money is often a touchy subject, so be respectful and flexible.

- **Know your priorities.** Really think about what's important to you. If it must be the hottest restaurant in town and it must be on a Saturday night in their busiest month, be prepared for extra costs and make adjustments elsewhere in the budget if necessary.

- **Choose your setting first.** All other decisions flow from knowing "where." Deciding that you'll be married at your parents' house in a tent gives you a completely different budget picture than if you had chosen a banquet hall or catering facility for your wedding.

- **Compare vendors**. Unless you have your heart set on one particular florist, restaurant, or photographer, obtain competitive bids and detailed descriptions of what's included from each. A hotel with built-in adjustable lighting has more value than one without. Know what you need from your vendors and be direct from the outset. If you'll want to rent linens, flowers, and lighting from your designer, make that clear right away. If you speak to two different tent companies, make sure

their proposals are for exactly the same equipment, labor, and services. Always compare apples to apples, and remember that the cheapest apple isn't necessarily the tastiest.

- **Make the most of your chosen location.** If they provide linens, tables, and chairs, try very hard to work with what is there. But do ask to see various options. Many facilities have several sets of china, a few types of chairs, and a range of linen styles or colors for you to choose from.

- **Whenever you can, be flexible.** Consider celebrating just before or after the season, day, or hour when your venue is busiest. You wanted yellow roses, but yellow dahlias are much less expensive in September—why not be perfectly in tune with nature *and* budget savvy?

- **Streamline your choices.** Instead of mixed arrangements, ask your florist to create all your centerpieces out of just one or two types of blossoms. Large volume purchases can mean discounts.

- **Stay true to your "mood."** If you're having a backyard wedding, limit the liquors you serve to white wine, punch, sparkling water, and a few microbrews. Serve from a buffet of homemade goodies. If you want a beautiful seafood buffet for your beach wedding, skip fancy hors d'oeuvres, and focus on luscious but simple presentation.

- **Trim the fat wherever possible.** This does not mean hiring fewer waiters than you need to serve your guests, or running out of champagne; it means looking for and modifying or eliminating areas that I call "highly optional." So, lose the pew swags and

focus on two absolutely beautiful altar arrangements. Limit the choices your guests have for hors d'oeuvres or entrées. Use cotton or polyester tablecloths instead of linen. If there's enough time, design your own invitations and place cards on the computer. And, of course, use your friends (but only the reliable ones) for favors whenever possible! You can repay them when *they* get married.

- **Don't forget to negotiate. Politely.** It's okay to ask for a reduction in costs, but make sure to take a positive approach, rather than questioning the value of something. I once had a client ask me why "putting together a few flower arrangements and a tablecloth or two" had to be so expensive when she already knew what colors and blossoms she liked. Without knowing what was involved, how could she understand that in addition to designing something beautiful, I had numerous meetings and handled a myriad of delivery, sourcing, and ordering details (her flowers were flown in from New Zealand). There was labor for preparation and setup, and all kinds of other costs. So don't insult your vendors by assuming that they're charging too much, but do feel free to ask them for explanations of charges and for recommendations about what could possibly be eliminated to help you save money. Honest professionals respect your need to stay within your budget, if you respect them too, you'll be able to work well together.

- **Plan for it now.** Booking services in advance is a great idea. Requesting everything in writing and keeping vendor estimates up-to-date as you move

through the process will keep "sticker shock" in check. Knowing that there are extra charges for things like extending your party time as well as cancelling reservations or damages, will keep you from panicking on your special day.

● **Remember: creativity trumps luxury.** Infuse your celebration with sentiment rather than a lavish display of stuff. Focus your budget and remember that a simple handwritten quote, a personal note to your guests, a well-crafted toast, even a single pretty flower in a well-placed vase will always be stylish, elegant, and meaningful.

Use seasonal flowers, en masse (above left). Ordering in quantity can result in discounts. And what is lovelier in May than a parade of pink peony bouquets? A basic glass vase or jar filled with purple anemones, surrounded by inexpensive votives, is perfect for winter or early spring (above right). Ask your florist for what's available.

ceremony
BASICS

Today's brides and grooms are exchanging vows in all kinds of wonderful places, from their childhood churches and temples to lush vineyards and funky lofts. I've designed ceremonies for couples in many different settings, from rolling lawns to quaint footbridges, from historic courtyards to industrial photo studios. Once I even created a ceremony space for a couple who wanted to exchange vows in the middle of a clothing and home-design boutique.

rows of rented white folding garden chairs are pretty (and practical) for an outdoor wedding. For this at-home ceremony, we anchored fluttery programs and petals for tossing with small river stones.

Your search for the right place to celebrate your commitment will be influenced by many factors, including your religious or spiritual beliefs, your families, where you met, the time of year, and other questions. Some couples pin down the location of the ceremony first, while others start with the reception venue, preferring to keep the entire celebration in one spot by finding a nearby house of worship or pretty park in which to say "I do."

Either way, once you've made your choice, you'll want to look at your ceremony with an eye toward meaning and simple beauty, focusing on what the location has to offer and on adorning your special space in a way that is lovely, reverential, festive, and romantic.

I always advise brides and grooms to keep their ceremony décor as simple as possible, avoiding giant sight-blocking aisle arches or cascading candelabras in favor of a focused approach that is more a thoughtful offering than an over-the-top extravaganza.

choosing your location

If your marriage will take place in a house of worship, visit the space at least once to view it from a design standpoint. Look at the scale and style of the architecture first. Is it gothic and ornate? Simple and spare? Modern or historic? Is it a space rich with ornamentation, murals, and varied colors? Or are there plenty of clean lines and a more monochromatic design? How high are the ceilings? Is appropriate lighting provided?

n this spectacular seaside setting, a simple, natural birch *huppah*, accented with breezy, sheer muslin panels and a woven cattail canopy, awaits the arrival of bride and groom.

If you'll exchange vows in a non-religious space such as a museum, loft, restaurant, or garden, look for the best place to have your ceremony—in front of a fireplace or between beautiful windows, or in the center of a flowering garden. Think about symmetry if you want to create a traditional aisle arrangement—or look for possibilities of doing the ceremony in the round, placing your *huppah* or a gazebo in the middle of an open space. Flow and access are also important—you'll want your guests and your bridal party to be able to enter the space with ease.

Here are some hints for designing your ceremony in a number of common locations.

HOUSES OF WORSHIP

- **Focus on the entrance and the altar area,** especially in a big space. Lots of aisle décor can add lots of expense and often obstructs your guests' view of the ceremony. Instead, opt for a single beautiful wreath, garland, or swag on or over the door and two scale-appropriate arrangements flanking the place where you'll stand.

- **Think of your décor as a tribute** honoring the day and your loved ones. Instead of decorating every pew or row of seats, just place small swags or wreaths on the rows where your immediate family will sit.

- **Ask about regulations.** Many times there is a list of rules—or even an approved vendor who is the only one permitted to decorate the space. You may only be allowed to decorate certain areas or might be required to use approved urns or

pedestals. Sometimes an aisle runner is not permitted. Find out how much time you'll have to set up and what, if anything, needs to be removed after the ceremony. Set this all out in writing with any florists or other vendors you hire to avoid extra charges and last-minute confusion.

- **Make your flowers an offering.** Instead of yanking your ceremony décor in a rush, and trying to gain double duty at the reception site, let your blossoms remain in this special place as a gesture of thanks and reverence. Some houses of worship will print a note in their service program with a dedication from you.

- **Consider a candle-lighting ceremony** if you'll be married in the evening. If permitted, this is an amazing way to bring light and romance to your space. Ask if the lights can be dimmed at a certain point. Together, each of you lights a single candle from a central "unity" flame, and then turns to light the candle of a member of your new spouse's family. They, in turn, light the candles of the guests next to them, and soon your ceremony is glimmering with soft, warm light. Ask your house of worship to recommend a vendor who sells candles and candle guards (paper or plastic rings which keep the hot wax from dripping).

- **If you'll be married in a warm month, ask about ventilation.** Most older spaces don't have air conditioning, but many have fans which can be turned on in advance to circulate air and many have windows which can be opened to let in a gentle breeze.

NEUTRAL INDOOR SPACES

- **Some public venues** have designated spaces where ceremonies often take place. If not, look for a beautiful view or a special architectural element, such as a fireplace or rotunda, to highlight. Remember that this area will be a backdrop for not only your vows, but also at least some of your pictures, so choose the spot carefully.

- **Consider color.** If the space is very white or neutral, you may want to choose one or two colors as accents for your flowers, aisle runners, etc. Recently, I designed a ceremony in a bright white Manhattan loft for a young couple who loved red. We made a simple *huppah* for their Jewish service out of red ilex berry branches and placed it in the center of a bank of windows facing the Hudson River. We used a wide red runner for the aisle and the bride ordered red suede yarmulkes for the men to wear during the service. Against the whiteness of the space, the red made such a beautiful contrast, and as the late afternoon sun set across the space, the groom (a composer, wearing a red tie) sang his bride (who wore a champagne-

There are no flowers in this ethereal ceremony held at New York City's Loft Eleven—just glowing pillar candles atop the mantel and in the fireplace, and two curvaceous candelabra bedecked with tall white tapers. The pretty aisle runner fabric was on sale at a discount fabric store. We simply unrolled the bolt, securing it with double-stick tape.

hued dress and carried red flowers) down the aisle. Simple and truly stunning.

- **If you will be using the same space for your reception,** choose décor that is easily moveable (or removable) to make for a quick turn-around transition. Pillar candle stands used to mark your aisle can be easily picked up and moved to your reception room after the ceremony, and the candlelight adds a wonderful romantic glow to the ceremony.

- **Be different.** Instead of a giant arch covered in flowers, place four simple pedestals around the perimeter of your sacred space, using clear glass cylinders or urns holding just one or two types of branches or flowers. These can be moved to the reception entrance or to your table or the dance floor during the reception.

- **Confirm with your designer** that staff will be on-site to rearrange, clean, and remove debris after the ceremony before your guests re-enter the space. Try to make sure that your guests don't see the turn-around process. Ask if the space can be blocked off, or if guests can enjoy cocktails in another space while the ceremony space is being transformed for dinner.

OUTDOOR SPACES

- **Plan for inclement weather.** Of course you *hope* the sun will be shining and the temperature will be just right. But you'll want to have a "Plan B" too, just in case. If you're tying the knot outside, make sure there is a place where you can be just as comfortable inside, so you won't be disappointed or flustered if the weather doesn't cooperate. Communicate the details of your Plan B to your florist, photographer, and musicians, so there won't be any confusion on the big day.

- **Keep décor modular and moveable.** If you've constructed a giant iron gazebo covered in three thousand peonies, you'd better plan for a tent to cover it, or you may find yourself without any ceremony décor at all if you're forced to move inside.

- **Use nature to your advantage.** Instead of flower arrangements, find two beautiful trees on the property to flank your ceremony. Stand on a clearing overlooking a lake, or in front of a row of grape vines. Mark your beach "aisle" with two rows of pretty shells or stones rather than ribbons and bows. Dunes, parks, and even backyard gardens are lovely places to have a natural, simple service. Never assume parks or landscaping will have flowers in bloom in your wedding month: ask in advance about colors and blooming seasons.

- **If your ceremony is in a public place,** organize your permits well in advance, and give a copy to the best man or a family member to keep on hand on the wedding day. Many parks, beaches, and historical sites have regulations for group gatherings and often there is a great demand for time slots, especially in warm months. Obtain printed lists of any regulations that apply and ask for recommendations for vendors who have worked at the site before.

- **Plan carefully for logistics.** Parking, wheelchair access, and directional signs for your guests must all be considered. Ask about these issues when you apply for permission to use the space.
- **Think about sound and sun.** If the ocean, a flowing fountain, or a bird sanctuary will be your backdrop, (or if your site is near an airport) you might want to hire a sound professional to provide wireless microphones. Your family and friends want to hear every word you speak! And be sure to check the location of the sun at your ceremony time to make certain your guests—and you—will not be staring straight into the glare.

creating a meaningful ceremony

Carefully chosen readings, quotations, music, and personal vows will add beauty and meaning to your wedding. Use your heritage, your shared passions, and your sense of humor as inspiration. After all, this is a celebration of the union of your two hearts and your two personalities—so proclaim them! This is your day.

And, remember that your bridal party is a joyful and colorful part of your celebration. A glowing bride and handsome groom, smiling bridesmaids in pretty dresses and dashing attendants with blooms or berries on their lapels: you will adorn your ceremony more beautifully than any form of decoration you can buy.

The Wedding of

Lisbeth Scott
and
Nathan William Barr

13 September

Greenwich, Co

This bride designed a vine and heart motif for her wedding, which took place at the groom's family home. The motif was used throughout the celebration as a personalizing detail. A program and handkerchief for happy tears (along with an envelope of tossing petals) awaited guests on each chair.

Logistics: **SIMPLE** | Décor: **SIMPLE** | Personalizing: **SIMPLE**

restaurant

The staff greets your guests with warmth and confidence, ushering them to festive tables set with antique silver or modern chopsticks. You toast your love with a fine champagne or delicate pinot noir, remembering the first time you dined here together. One by one, your favorite foods are placed before you and your guests in the glowing candlelight. And to think that you planned all this in just a few brief meetings! A restaurant reception offers instant style, easy planning, and lots of extras. If you truly want your celebration to be simple, holding it in a restaurant is a great idea.

deliciously simple

Restaurants offer many advantages and so much variety in the way of hospitality, design, and, of course, great food and wine. There are casual dim sum dining halls, cozy romantic bistros, cutting-edge temples of gastronomy, and flashy celebrity haunts—the trick is choosing your perfect cuisine, location, and atmosphere.

New York City's Django restaurant, designed by David Rockwell, was the setting for this wedding feast. Tables arranged in long lines, with sufficient space between them, made it easier for guests to be seated. We used the restaurant's plates, glasses, and furniture, and simply added fabric overlays, a few bud vases, tea lights, and an accent flower for each napkin.

If you're serious food-lovers, hosting your wedding in a restaurant can be an opportunity to have a great chef cook a once-in-a-lifetime feast for you, your family, and your friends. In addition, if you're a practical, super-simple or budget-conscious couple, you'll find many of the elements you need and want for your celebration already provided in most restaurant settings. Unlike a tent, loft, or outdoor space, a restaurant almost always has chairs, tables, good lighting, a full bar, a kitchen, coat-check facilities, and an experienced staff. Many times even flowers, music, candles, and parking are included.

Often there will also be a professional banquet or wedding manager on site to help you coordinate details and make choices.

Another important detail: unlike a wedding at an event space, restaurant service and kitchen staff are always "at home" in the venue, which is adapted to the needs and specifications of their cuisine. This can be a very important advantage when it comes to ease of planning and consistency of food preparation.

I recently designed a restaurant ceremony and reception for a couple who were on a limited budget. They chose a sleek, modern place near Manhattan's Central Park. This stylish couple picked the restaurant as much for its wonderful food as for its contemporary design, and they found that almost everything they wanted was included: gorgeous chairs, a beautiful staircase, high-quality linens—even a doorman.

To enhance the space and create a sense of reverence for the ceremony, I suggested a few key floral arrangements, with lines of white candles and a sheer, billowy curtain to hide an unattractive corner of the room. When the couple decided they had to cut out votive candles to lower their budget, the restaurant manager volunteered to throw them in at no additional charge, because he had a large quantity in stock. The lucky bride and groom walked into the space on their wedding day to find it glowing with over 200 simple votive candles—and the restaurant picked up the cost of the curtain as well, noting that it would be a good thing to have on-site for future parties.

inspiration

COLORS: Look to the space for clues. For light spaces, choose whites or greens, lemon yellows, or vibrant hues. For darker rooms, opt for rich tones in wine, orange, plum, or chocolate.

FLOWERS: Herbs, non-fragrant blooms, fruits, and vegetables. Wildflowers for more casual spaces; orchids or calla lilies for modern rooms, or sculpted roses and berries in more formal settings.

MATERIALS: Fine papers, spices, simple bud vases, fabric runners.

HOW IT FEELS: Convivial, organized, warm, festive, intimate, delicious, all-inclusive.

CROSS-REFERENCE: See the Vineyard, Hotel and Private Club chapters for more advice.

If your restaurant tables are narrow, use simple bud vases with just one or two blossoms, like these cheerful white dahlias (above). Choose a space with interesting details and décor, such as a candlelit bar for cocktail hour, or a sexy lounge for your after-party (opposite).

The point is that restaurants are often generous, flexible, and very service-oriented. They might pitch in to help stuff gift bags for your favors or tailor a signature dish to your wishes without charging you extra. Another bride I worked with had been married in a formal traditional ceremony in her native Morocco. She and her groom had planned a festive party at a hip downtown New York City restaurant for their return. At our menu meeting a week before the reception, the restaurant's chefs were extremely accommodating and eager-to-please. When the bride asked how she could decorate an inexpensive plastic tiered stand she wanted to use to display traditional homemade desserts, the pastry chef offered to *airbrush it in chocolate* at no extra charge. It was beautiful!

When the same bride had trouble choosing from all the luscious desserts offered, the pastry chef suggested they make smaller versions of *all* the sweets so that guests could try everything. Although this bride had chosen not to spend her budget on table linens, when my staff arrived to set up the space, a team of waiters magically appeared with yards and yards of luxurious fabric which we used to drape the sumptuous buffet table.

Of course, you can't plan for or count on these extras being provided, nor should you demand them. But if you're flexible and inquisitive, you just might get more for your money than you'd think.

In addition to great cooks, restaurants have host and management staff who are experts at planning and rearranging their spaces, and at knowing what you need to know to make the day or evening flow as smoothly as possible. Often, they act as a sort of day-of-wedding coordinator, helping you to stay on schedule and dealing with any last-minute issues or requests. Throughout your planning process, they may be able to help you with recommendations about layouts and details which work well in the space, or with vendors and other service providers who are familiar with the location and its special features and needs.

Some of the most intimate weddings I have attended have been in restaurants, as they are often best suited to smaller groups. They also offer a special place to return to for anniversaries and other important celebrations. I was dining in a charming restaurant recently when I overheard two couples at different tables strike up a conversation. One couple, had been married at the restaurant exactly a year earlier. The other couple was celebrating their 30th anniversary, as a gift from their daughter, who had been married in this romantic spot. Both couples were now a part of this restaurant's "family."

The most important thing to consider in a restaurant, aside from appropriate size, is how well it fits your style. So many restaurants today are on the cutting edge of design and cuisine—just find one that is perfect for you! Look for beautiful (yet comfortable) chairs, appealing colors, and a menu which reflects your preferences.

I advise choosing your restaurant first for the quality of its food and service, as a well-attended and well-fed guest is a happy guest. If you are a design-oriented couple, you can take it to the next level by looking for a venue with unique style. Details to look for include candles, adjustable lighting, and fine china and glassware. Also look at the flow from space to space if you'll be hosting the ceremony, cocktails, and dinner all in the restaurant.

Once you've chosen the perfect place, be it a trattoria, a bistro or an asian-inspired eatery, take the restaurant's spirit and run with it. Create your invitations and guest favors to fit the theme.

know your setting

● **All restaurants have busier times** of the week, month, and year. For example, a restaurant with a garden might charge a premium for a summer outdoor wedding, while a cozy tavern with a fireplace might be booked solid in the winter months. If you're planning to take over the whole space, you may get a better deal if you can work around their schedule. On the other hand, some establishments are closed for lunch or dinner on certain days and may be eager to book those times for additional revenue without having to turn away regular guests. Ask what's available.

django has a small, Moroccan-style tented dining area, perfect for an after-dinner sweets lounge. Pastry Chef Nancy Olson created a buffet of confections which could be enjoyed at the wedding, or packed up for later in the gift boxes provided. Baker Cheryl Kleinman referred to swatches of textiles to design the wedding cake, which appears on page 49.

● **Restaurants are generally best** for small- to medium-sized celebrations. Many offer private dining rooms for varying numbers of guests, allowing you to rent a part of the space for your party without having to pay the costs of closing the restaurant completely for the day or evening.

Make sure to let management know if you're planning dancing or entertainment, as this will affect the amount of space you'll need, and possibly, other diners. And be sure to introduce any wedding day vendors to the appropriate contact person, so they can be clear about delivery instructions, power requirements, etc.

- **If you will be doing additional decorating,** or setting up musical equipment, ask about setup and break-down times. Many restaurants book parties for specific time periods and will charge extra if staff must come in early or stay late, or if they must curtail a service period to accommodate your request.

- **If you will have your ceremony in the dining room,** ask for help in determining how the transition from vows to cocktails and dinner will take place. Inquire if there's a terrace, another room, or a mezzanine where guests can relax and enjoy hors d'oeuvres while the staff prepares the room for dinner.

- **If you will hold your ceremony in the restaurant,** ask the manager or maitre d' to halt service and any noisy kitchen preparations during your vows. I once saw a restaurant wedding

Choose a restaurant with foods you love, beautifully presented. Whether yours is a buffet-style celebration or a formal sit-down affair, pay attention to details and the artful arrangement of your wedding dishes. Chef Cedric Tovar's special menu included a scallop appetizer with corn foam.

interrupted by waiters who were enthusiastically filling water glasses with ice in the back of the room. Clink! Clink! Clink! You don't want staff walking, talking, or working anywhere near your ceremony space.

- **Ask how the restaurant is best configured.** Look at a floor plan created for a similar-sized party. Confirm that the restaurant has held at least a few weddings before, and that the tables will be arranged in a way that works for you. Call couples who've held weddings there for references and tips.

keep it simple and stunning

- **Choose a restaurant that is suited to your style.** If you're casual, pick a trattoria or a bistro with a patio or garden: if you're serious "foodies," consider spending more for a smaller number of guests and host an amazing feast. Consult friends and local guidebooks, or rent your favorite neighborhood spot, or a place that has special meaning for the two of you.

- **Eat in the restaurant several times** before you sign a contract, to make sure it's right for your celebration. Share any comments or expectations with the manager or maitre d' so you won't have any surprises at the last minute.

- **Meet the chef.** Let him know how much you enjoy his food. Tell him your favorites, but avoid dictating a menu. You'd be surprised how generous most chefs are when it comes to pleasing valued customers, especially ones who love the restaurant enough to celebrate a wedding there.

- **Pick a restaurant that already has service ware** and the decorative touches you like. You will save a lot of money if you don't have to rent all the accoutrements.

- **If the restaurant has fresh flowers,** ask if you can speak to their designer in advance of the wedding. Many times you can make special requests or pay a supplement to have the flowers tailored to your wishes. If you can't afford extra flowers, ask if the restaurant will supply a simple bowl filled with green apples or purple potatoes, or just lots of candles for each table.

- **Request that any fake flowers** or unsuitable décor be removed on the day of your wedding. Feel free to ask for a special napkin fold or other modifications to existing décor.

- **Find out how tables will be configured** for your party. Often restaurants simply push tables together, which can make for uneven tabletops. Ask how many servers will be allotted for your party. Make it clear to be sure that your guests will be comfortable and well cared-for.

- **Ask whether the restaurant can help** with a personalized favor, such as a box of handmade chocolates. Have waiters serve them on elegant or fun trays.

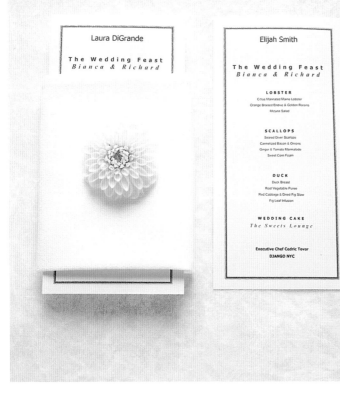

- **Specify your lighting requests.** Almost all restaurants have lighting on adjustable systems, which makes it easy to create just the mood you want. Many have candles on every table. Request extra candles for tables, the bar, the buffet, etc., if your wedding is in the evening.

- **Ask to have a special menu printed** for your wedding. Many restaurants print their menus daily or seasonally on their own computers and can customize yours with a special heading of your choice. Consider printing or lettering the menus with your guests' names to create a unique place card and memento.

where to splurge

- **Serve special and luxurious foods and wines.** In addition to the standard chicken and salmon, choose a wild game option, followed by a cheese course. Or ask for a traditional Japanese *kaiseki* tasting menu and a sake sampling. Select an Austrian Riesling rather than a chardonnay, and offer a special sweet wine with your cake or dessert.

- **Use fine linens.** Most restaurants use standard polyester-cotton blend tablecloths and napkins, which are fine for everyday, but you might want something more special (or something floor-length) for your wedding. Ask what your options are, and consider calling a local rental company

reality check

- Never plan to hold your wedding in a brand-new restaurant. I once designed a last-minute celebration for a prominent food writer who had booked the hottest new just-about-to-open spot in Grand Central Station. When the opening date was pushed back beyond her wedding day, she got her deposit back, but all her invitations had been mailed, and a new location had to be found!

- Don't bring your own wine (or cake, or anything to eat or drink, for that matter) without advance clearance from the establishment. Many restaurants charge extra for such additions, in the form of "corkage" or cake "plating" fees.

- Avoid creating "cash bar" or other premium liquor charges for your guests. Many fine restaurants carry grappas, vintage ports, single-malt Scotch whiskeys, and even Sauternes, which may cost extra. Negotiate what is included in your per-guest price. Then, ask to have any not included items removed from sight, so as to avoid guests feeling embarrassed.

- Avoid highly fragrant flowers and scented candles, which can interfere with the aromas of your fine foods and wines.

for available styles. Just make sure to obtain a written list of table sizes from the restaurant so you'll know what to order.

- **Hire musicians appropriate to the setting.** You might find an accordionist to play French love songs during cocktails in your bistro, or an opera trio to serenade you between antipasti and fettucine if you're dining Italian-style.

a restaurant is the perfect place to create a signature cocktail to match your wedding mood (above). This hibiscus-infused libation is named "The Passionflower." Menus, personalized with guests' names, were printed out with a computer (opposite, above). A bolt of non-fraying crushed velour trimmed to the table's length makes for an instant, inexpensive table overlay (opposite, below).

Logistics: **SIMPLE** | Décor: **SIMPLE** | Personalizing: **MODERATE**

private club

You greet your guests under a crystal chandelier, while white-gloved waiters serve classic drinks and offer caviar from an elegantly carved ice bar. Your hand-lettered wedding monogram adorns programs, menus, even your cake, and luxurious damask linens grace your tables. A sense of tradition and history fills the halls as you dine and dance to a live orchestra in the grand ballroom, surrounded by those you love.

exclusively yours

There are many reasons to be married at a private club if the idea suits you. Many offer historic architecture, full catering facilities, impeccable service, and the amenities associated with the finest hotels. All this makes a private club wedding one of the simplest to plan. There is also the "posh" factor to be considered—after all, an exclusive club is a glamorous address on your wedding invitation.

There are many types of private clubs that are well-equipped to host wedding celebrations. We've chosen to feature the exquisite Westchester Country Club in Rye, New York, for its romantic interior, but excellent settings can be found among university clubs, boating clubs, and many other historic associations all across the country.

If you choose a country club setting, you might host tennis or golf round-robins, and swimming parties for the kids. If there's a health spa within the club, perhaps you might offer a relaxing yoga class for the ladies.

the Westchester Country Club, in Rye, New York, was the backdrop for this classical ceremony. The vow space was set amid three soaring windows, with classical urn arrangements of ivory French tulips placed on pedestals. Rented bamboo chairs are accented with simple cotton covers, and the aisle runner is made from inexpensive lace.

In the same spirit, a yacht or boating club would be ideal for a clambake or lobster feast with simple gingham table linens and breezy aperitifs or microbrews.

If you're more of a metropolitan club couple, use your venue as an inspiration to create a sophisticated, vintage-style celebration in the grand tradition of white tie and tails, civilized cocktails, caviar, and the sounds of a great orchestra.

There is much to consider when thinking about a private club wedding. First and foremost is whether you, or someone you know, has a membership. Private clubs are exclusive facilities with a wide range of criteria for deciding who can hold an event on-site. Rates and permissions (as well as preferred dates) may be more accessible to those who are already members, but many clubs offer sponsorships, where an existing member may, in effect, "host" the event to allow others to make use of the facilities.

The fact is that while clubs thrive on their exclusive membership, they often wish to supplement income and the use of their banquet rooms with parties paid for and hosted by nonmembers. So don't be discouraged if you're not a member of a club where you'd like to celebrate—just contact their events office and inquire about what's possible.

You will want to find out right away what's associated with holding your wedding at a given club. Donations may be required, timing and dates may be limited, and there may even be restrictions on your use of the club's name and address in printed materials or public announcements.

EXCLUSIVE
inspiration

COLORS: In historical club settings, opt for sophisticated combinations. Look at your surroundings: for dark wood spaces, consider ivory or white as your base color, accenting with chocolate, burgundy, navy, even yellow or red. For lighter rooms, choose ethereal colors—pastels, whites, and ivories.

FLOWERS: Masses of roses, fruits, hydrangea, ivy, Queen Anne's lace, stock, ranunculus, peonies, seasonal leaves and greens.

MATERIALS: Silver, linen, velvet, lace, taffeta, julep cups, Revere bowls, antiques.

HOW IT FEELS: Swanky, conservative, classic, formal, elegant.

CROSS-REFERENCE: See the Hotel, Restaurant, and Contry Inn chapters for more ideas and advice.

know your setting

● **Private clubs do not often advertise** their banquet or ballroom facilities, even though they might be available for public use under certain circumstances. Instead, they rely on word-of-mouth and referrals, so ask around and make calls to clubs you're considering, even if you think they might be "members-only."

Silver compotes hold mixed arrangements of blossoms in white and green. The club provided fine silver and plateware for the tables, which were accented with rented ivory damask linens and pearl napkin rings. Crystal taper candlesticks complement the grand crystal chandeliers.

- **On any given date,** a club facility might host numerous different events, including multiple weddings. Inquire before booking, and ask about start times, staffing, and the proximity of other celebrations to make sure you guests won't be affected.

- **The majority of private clubs** have their own in-house catering staff and kitchens. Often, outside caterers are discouraged or even prohibited. Ask to schedule a tasting before booking if possible (even if you must pay for it), to be certain you like the food.

keep it simple and stunning

- **Use everything you can** that the club has to offer. Many have crested china patterns and high-quality silver and linens. Ask to see various options (often there are several) and take advantage of the best they have.

- **Take a good look around the club** from a decorative perspective. If there are elements which seem inappropriate for your party décor, such as artificial plants or flowers, inquire whether they can be relocated during your wedding celebration.

- **If you are in an historic club,** ask the chef to create a vintage menu for your party and build your reception around a classic theme.

- **Unlike many other venues,** clubs often have an abundance of interesting rooms and gathering spaces. Take advantage of this to create an easy flow and eye-pleasing visual change for your celebration, perhaps using one room for the ceremony, a second for cocktails, a ballroom for dinner, and a reading room or study for cognacs and ports later in the evening. This eliminates the need to "flip" spaces quickly to accommodate the next stage of your party, and allows guests to enjoy as much of the club as possible. It's worth negotiating on this point, so give it a try!

- **If you are in a modern club environment,** you may find yourself in a space decorated like a corporate-style hotel. If so, focus on lighting, including table pin-spots to highlight flowers, and use as many candles as possible.

- **Clubs almost always have beautiful pieces** of furniture. Find an antique table near the entrance and use it to display photographs of the two of you—or even vintage family wedding portraits—as a warm, personal welcome. (Be sure to put some-one you trust in charge of retrieving and packing up these precious photos at the end of the party.)

- **Create a classic crest or monogram** for your wedding and use it on all your printed materials, from invitations to programs, even on your cake and thank-you notes.

- **Embrace your surroundings.** If you are in a formal, traditional setting, celebrate tradition with pristine silver Revere bowls or mint julep

graphic designer Judith Ness created the vintage-style monogram that appears on the wedding program (page 60), the menus (opposite, above), and even the cake (page 68). Every printed piece, from menus and programs, to escort cards (see page 60), and even table numbers, are hand-lettered. The latter were placed in decorative frames, which now adorn the bride's new home (opposite, below).

cups filled with saucer-sized roses or gracious lilacs for a timeless, elegant effect. Stay away from minimalist or "pop" contemporary designs.

● **If you'll be staying at the club** on your wedding night, ask your florist to decorate your room with flowers and candles while you're celebrating. Since he will already be on-site, you won't have to pay for an extra delivery charge.

where to splurge

● **Coordinate linens with your architecture.** Choose fancy Victorian prints or elegant damasks, even toiles, for fabulous effect.

● **Ask the club's pastry chef to make individual wedding cakes** (or cake-shaped cookies) for each guest, with the club's crest emblazoned in icing, along with your monogram and wedding date.

● **Have everything hand-lettered,** vintage-style, from invitations to menus.

● **Serve the world's finest cognacs,** ports, and cigars after dinner, with engraved silver cigar-cutters and personalized cigar matchboxes for your guests.

● **Skip the deejay** and opt for a 20-piece orchestra or big band—true glamour!

● **Hire professional ballroom dancers** to circulate throughout the party. And of course, make sure you've had a few lessons together so you can fox-trot the night away.

xecutive Chef Edward Leonard designed a classic club menu of luxury foods (above, left). Private clubs often have skilled staff who can create ice sculptures, like this one for a caviar and vodka bar (above, right). Baker Colette Peters of Colette's Cakes accented this cake with a vintage-style bowl cake topper filled with sugar stephanotis, using a monogram for inspiration (opposite).

Logistics: **MODERATE** | Décor: **SIMPLE** | Personalizing: **SIMPLE**

country inn

You and your bridal party check in early to greet your guests for a barbecue rehearsal dinner. Tomorrow you'll be married on the lawn and celebrate with dinner in an antique-filled dining room set with beautiful china, old silver, and cut crystal glassware. On Sunday, you'll host a farewell brunch on the gracious porch. Your charming country inn becomes a cozy homestead for a beautiful weekend of romance and family.

warmth and charm

Country inns are magical places, filled with history and designed for comfort. They're often owned or managed by highly creative hosts with a flair for design and a penchant for entertaining. If you're inclined to celebrate your wedding at an inn, you likely envision a warm, cozy celebration, whether formal or more casual.

Inns come in all shapes and sizes and are situated in every kind of setting, from townhouse to mansion, from castle to ranch house to farm to former plantation. Often they were once taverns on the only main road through an historic town. Sometimes they are converted private estates which have been renovated to feature whirlpool baths, fine linens, and amenities such as spa treatments and award-winning restaurants.

If you're searching for the perfect inn, you'll want to consider whether you'll just host your reception there, or whether you'll make a wedding weekend out of it, taking rooms for your bridal party and creating a series of events pre- and post-wedding. Many lovely inns feature built-in ceremony spots such as gazebos and gardens, complete with giant stone fireplaces and wrap-around porches and they are often smaller and more intimate than a standard hotel.

Some inns offer wonderful weekend packages which can save you money and planning time—after

or this weekend wedding, set at Willow Grove Inn, in Orange, Virginia, we decked the inn's doors with a lush welcome garland of lemon leaf and roses, and two simple swags of "Virginia" roses (above). Inns are wonderful places to hold the smaller parties which surround your celebration, such as a cozy rehearsal dinner, or this sunny post-wedding brunch (opposite).

all, if you host all or most of your satellite parties and your wedding in one location, you have the advantage of staying in one place, cozy and comfortable, as well as the benefit of having a single staff to coordinate everything.

You might live in an area where there are a number of fine inns to consider. Take a weekend afternoon to explore several possibilities, and make appointments to talk with staff and gather brochures, menus, and pricing information for rooms and banquet packages.

If you want to make your wedding a "weekend getaway" event for your guests, use the Internet or local chamber of commerce resources to help point you in the right direction. There are many great websites about inns, complete with photos, rate information, and descriptions of the properties and their amenities.

Certain inns, especially those based in historic homes, have smaller connected rooms for dining, while others have renovated or added larger banquet-style facilities or even tent structures to accommodate larger groups. Inquire about possibilities for your party size to make sure you've got the right fit.

Whichever type of inn you choose, make the most of the architectural elements and decorative touches throughout your spaces. If there is a beautiful porch or parlor, ask about hosting some part of your celebration there. Center your ceremony or an after-dinner lounge around a warm fireplace in colder months. Mix-and-match china patterns, linens, and antique chairs and tables

INN

inspiration

COLORS: Take clues from the interior and the architecture—opt for antique-style print tablecloths such as damasks and toiles, in bold or soft colors.

FLOWERS: Garden roses, delphinium, snapdragons, ranunculus, tulips, autumn leaves, fruits, holiday greens and garlands.

MATERIALS: Silver, porcelain, fine paper, brass, wood, lace, baskets, taper candles.

HOW IT FEELS: Cozy, warm, historic, homey, one-of-a-kind.

CROSS-REFERENCE: The Farm, Vinyard, and Restaurant offer good advice for both logistics and design.

or a holiday wedding, you can incorporate winter greens, or clusters of pretty ornaments in your floral arrangements (above). Willow Grove's collection of antique silver, china, and chairs was used for the dinner tables at this wedding. A variety of roses in antique teapots and rented brocade linens for the tables complemented the inn's interior (opposite).

can add a wonderful sense of history, romance, and character to your wedding, so try to use them wherever possible.

Many innkeepers, especially those who own smaller properties, tend to be very creative and design-oriented, often interested in history and preservation. They might work with local florists to decorate their public rooms throughout the year, and chances are they know what styles and colors best suit their spaces. Enlist their help when planning your own décor, and think about incorporating a drawing or historical photograph of the property into

your printed materials, such as save-the-date cards, invitations, programs, and menus.

Whether your inn is tavern-like and casual or more ornate and formal, look to its spirit and surroundings to inspire your wedding details. Hosting your wedding at a country inn is like celebrating at the home of a gracious friend who is known for her entertaining style. Let the beauty and warmth of this special place infuse your wedding day with classic charm and timeless hospitality.

know your setting

- **Inns are usually in historic spaces,** and often in tourist destinations. Arrange for transportation and hotel accommodations, and provide good, clear directions for your guests.

- **Some inns require you to reserve** the entire space or a large block of rooms as a part of your package. Ask for brochures, pricing information, and any restrictions up-front, and make sure to read your contract carefully for details.

- **Inns, like most great destinations,** have on- and off-seasons. Some are busiest during warmer months; others may be more popular during the holidays. If you want to save money and gain more personal attention, consider hosting your wedding pre- or post-season.

- **One great benefit** of taking over an entire inn is that it becomes your home for the night or weekend. If you won't have exclusive use of the inn ask how your party might impact other guests, or how they might impact your party.

- **Popular inns book up** well in advance. Some as far as six months to a year ahead. Don't wait to secure your date!

keep it simple and stunning

- **Make use of what the inn has available**—an antique table to hold your escort cards, eclectic china for your tables, holiday décor to accent your party.
- **Mix antique linen prints or textures** in one color, such as ivory or burgundy.
- **Use flea-market finds** for flower containers and give them away as favors.
- **Negotiate a weekend package**—most inns are privately owned and management might be happy to offer a discount for a series of events.
- **Create a welcome gift** that features local snacks or wines, and include an itinerary for the weekend with suggested activities. Ask the inn for help coordinating sightseeing visits, a round of golf, or an antiquing trip for your guests.
- **Use a picture of the inn** on your invitations, programs, favors, or welcome cards. This is a great way to personalize your celebration.

reality check

- As with any wedding, make sure to have transportation available for any guests who've done "a bit too much" celebrating.

- Visit the inn, and consider staying overnight at least once before the wedding. Try the food, services, and accommodations so you'll know what to expect and what to request for your guests.

- Because inns are in older spaces, some with antique windows and electrical systems, there may be complications with air conditioning, heat, hot water, or other comfort concerns. Most reputable inns have their guests' comfort as their utmost objective, but it never hurts to inquire about these things in advance.

- Ask for references from other couples who've married at your prospective inn. It never hurts to seek advice from those who've gone before you.

Willow Grove owner Angela Mulloy made this Spirited Groom's Cake, a nutty, chocolate, bourbon-infused confection that can be a companion to the wedding cake or a dessert for the rehearsal dinner (opposite, above). After dinner, spiced nuts, bourbons, and fine cognacs were served in a cigar lounge in the parlor (opposite, below).

- **Base your wedding menu on** an historic dinner, or on local, seasonal favorites.
- **Decorate the inn.** Add a garland or wreath to the front door or the banquet facility to create a warm welcome.
- **Many inns have cookbooks** or other souvenirs which make great favors. Consider personalizing your gifts with a keepsake from your inn.

where to splurge

- **Spend your entire** wedding week at the inn, relaxing, reading, and preparing to greet your guests.
- **Hire a musical ensemble** to play at your cocktail hour—if you're in a Victorian setting, hire a classical trio. If your inn is a castle, think baroque. If you'll celebrate in a Mission-style inn, hire a Spanish or Mexican group to serenade you.
- **Adorn all the balconies or windows** of the inn with flower-filled garlands.
- **If permitted, host your wedding dinner** entirely by candlelight, as they would have centuries ago. What could be more romantic? (Just make sure to take extra safety precautions.)
- **Have fresh flowers arranged and placed** in each guest room as a fragrant welcome.
- **Have your bridal suite filled with flowers.** Ask your florist to take care of this while your party is in progress, or ask the inn staff to move centerpieces up to your room as the party winds down.

make a wedding weekend out of it. Reserve the whole inn and welcome your guests with local treats and an itinerary that lets them know what's happening, and when and where (above). Your inn can be your wedding home and headquarters. This bride's dress and lily-of-the-valley bouquet await her in the former summer kitchen at Willow Grove (opposite).

Logistics: **MODERATE** | Décor: **SIMPLE** | Personalizing: **SIMPLE**

vineyard

Long, perfect rows of winding, leafy vines preside over your ceremony. The cocktail hour offers an elegant tasting of seasonal food and wine pairings served al fresco as the sun sets. Dinner is laid out like a feast among the grapes or in a cozy cellar, and a special cuvée of your favorite wine awaits each guest as an elegant, delicious souvenir. Let the toasting begin!

a toast to love

The spirit of a vineyard wedding (no pun intended) is one of both conviviality and connoisseurship. There is something inherently festive about a vineyard event, and a connection to seasonal, modern celebrations as

a bouquet of roses and hypericum berries is as lush as a cabernet vineyard in September (above). This vineyard wedding, set at the Wölffer Estate in Sagaponack, New York, featured a simple, grape-accented ceremony in a gazebo nestled among the vines (opposite).

well as the historic festivals of the ancient world, where wine has been celebrated since 1000 B.C.

Couples who choose to celebrate in a vineyard generally want a natural setting, but a sophisticated atmosphere. Vineyards are farms, after all, but they also have a certain cachet because of their association with fine wines, foods, and the noblest sort of agriculture.

In the United States, vineyard weddings are often "destination" weddings where guests might be invited for a weekend of festivities. Abroad, you might celebrate your wedding along the Strada del Vino in Italy's Alto Adige region, or in a fantastic chateau in France's Chateauneuf-du-Pape. Spain, New Zealand, Germany, Portugal—all have well-established wine-producing areas to investigate, as do many other wonderful spots.

More and more, vineyards and wineries are springing up all over the map. Oregon, Washington, and New York State, as well as Chile and Argentina, are examples of areas that are at the forefront of the newest high-caliber selections. Deciding where you want your vineyard wedding to take place will be determined by your preference, the size of your guest list, and your budget.

Chances are if there are vineyards in your area, you already know some of them. Whether you'll celebrate close to home or in another part of the country or world, you can use the Internet and some of the great wine and travel magazines to conduct your research, along with the honeymoon sections of bridal magazines. Gather brochures and make plans to visit your favorite vineyards.

inspiration

COLORS: Stay natural. Use grape colors, whites and ivories, or other fruit- or vegetable-inspired shades.

FLOWERS: Why not use grapes, cheeses, olives, and just a few blooms? If you're a flower lover, stick to non-fragrant seasonal blossoms, such as sunflowers, roses, or dahlias.

MATERIALS: Ceramics, fine papers, wrought iron, fine linen, tile, wood.

HOW IT FEELS: Gourmet, sophisticated, natural, convivial, festive, bacchanalian.

CROSS-REFERENCE: See the Farm, Restaurant, Tent, and Country Inn chapters for more inspiration.

Most vineyards that host weddings are associated with a caterer, or even a variety of catering companies. Many vineyards will work with only the best vendors in the business, which can increase your cost, but will generally also increase the quality of the food. And if you're like most wine-loving couples, you're probably also food enthusiasts, so the matching of foods and wines might be of special importance to you.

Then again, you might just enjoy the beauty and natural elegance of a vineyard atmosphere. Either way, make sure to research your options. Take a "planning weekend" getaway to visit vineyards you're considering.

ayer your celebration with thematic details. This cake, by Buddy Valastro of Carlo's Bakery in Hoboken, New Jersey, is accented with sugar grape clusters (above). We arranged long, feast-like tables next to the vines, and used a deep palette of burgundies paired with ivory accents. The bride's and groom's chairs, at the head of the table, are adorned with special covers and grapes (opposite).

know
your flow

While you're looking for a suitable vineyard, you'll want to consider the layout and flow of your event from start to finish. If you'll hold the ceremony on-site, where will it take place and what is the rain plan? How will guests move between ceremony, cocktail hour, and dinner? Is there a way to use different parts of the facility for different stages of the wedding? For example, could cocktails be held outdoors in nice weather, with dinner taking place inside a tasting room or banquet facility?

What a vineyard provides, unlike a tent or a loft space, is instant atmosphere. Barrels, vines, pretty glasses and bottles, architectural details—they're all already in place, which makes it easier to create a celebration which is both simple and stunning.

You can use what the vineyard has to offer to make your wedding easier, or more elegant and unique. We gathered grapes, breadsticks, and just a few flowers to create centerpieces for our long tables, accented by pillar candles under hurricane glass shades to protect them from the wind. The winery had large, dramatic candelabra which could be used at the entrance or to line a hallway or path.

Think of your vineyard as a wonderful pairing of farm and restaurant. Take advantage of the beauty that surrounds you to create a magical feast for your wedding day.

know your setting

- **Every vineyard is different.** Some are merely properties that grow and harvest grapes to be sold and used by outside wineries; others do everything on-site. You will want to take a tour of the facility before deciding if it's right for you.

- **Most vineyards that host events** have a planning staff to help you make arrangements. Ask them what works best. Obtain a floor plan for any areas you are considering using, and study the flow to and from various spaces. Also keep in mind your alternatives should the weather be inclement.

- **As at any farm,** you'll want to know if there will be any disruptive noise on your wedding day, or any other activities that might affect your celebration. Ask about odors as well. (Fermenting grapes can sometimes create unpleasant smells.)

- **Many vineyards and wineries** are open to the public for daily tastings and tours. Find out whether this will be the case on your wedding day. I recently attended a winery wedding where people kept opening the front door and walking into the middle of the ceremony! Make sure this won't happen on your big day.

- **Consider your season.** A vineyard looks very different in April than in early September, when the grapes are full-grown and the vines are full of leaves. Try to visit the setting in your wedding season so you'll know what to expect.

reality check

- I strongly recommend providing, or at least organizing, transportation for any guests who may imbibe a wee bit too much of the delicious wine you're offering. Their sincere desire to taste everything may overwhelm their ability to get themselves home safely.

- Make sure to secure advance permission for any outside wines or spirits you might want to bring in for your wedding. Some wineries will serve only their own wines, while others will be more flexible.

- As with any outdoor wedding, ask the vineyard staff about any problem insects such as bees and mosquitoes, and make sure to have insect repellent on hand for your guests.

- In addition to your guests, consider protecting any exposed foods or beverages (especially sugary cakes and punch drinks) from outdoor pests.

Instead of lots of flowers, we filled dark metal urns and compotes with grapes and breadsticks, and tucked them next to wind-resistant glass hurricane candle shades holding pillar candles. Half-bottles of Wölffer Estate wine "La Ferme" merlot were both guest favors and place cards, with personalized hang tags designed by Kristina Wrenn. For napkin rings, we folded a piece of paper around each napkin, then added a wax seal with the couple's initial (page 80).

keep it simple and stunning

- **Layer your celebration with details** that relate to the winery, or to wine and grapes. Use a grape motif or an etching of the winery as an accent on your invitations, cocktail napkins, programs, or place cards.

- **Host a "tasting hour"** instead of the traditional cocktail hour. Acclaimed Hamptons caterer Janet O'Brien helped us create bite-sized hors d'oeuvres served on trays with small tastes of wines that paired perfectly with her seasonal ingredients.

- **Avoid big, fancy flower decorations.** Instead, use a beautiful vine-covered spot on the property for your ceremony.

- **Ask your caterer to bring extra grapes,** and display bread baskets and breadsticks, nuts, olives, and other edible elements in the center of the table as guests are seated. This will be a tasty, unique, and less costly welcome for your guests!

- **Match your wines to your menu,** and list the wines served next to or under each dish. Your guests might fall in love with one of your great pairings and want to order a case to take home.

- **Stay passionate, or at least natural,** with your color story. Avoid pastels and "pop" colors in favor of muted, deep, or vibrant tones. Choose

his centerpiece uses a lighter color palette. Grapes, roses, and breadsticks are arranged in ceramic urns (above). A vineyard is the perfect place to offer special liqueurs, from grappas and ports to sweet wines (opposite, above). For the cocktail hour, caterer Janet O'Brien created "tastings" of bite-sized hors d'oeuvres served with just a sip of wine (opposite, below).

linens that feature a vine motif or a grape-inspired color rather than fancy damasks. Stay away from shiny or sparkly decorations and opt for organic elements instead.

- **Choose a fun party favor**—a split of wine, a wine-tasting book, a corkscrew, a bottle of wine vinegar, or some other wine-related item will surely be a hit.

where to splurge

- **Ask the winemaker to create a** special Wedding Cuvée just for you. Serve it with dinner or for a special toast, and give a bottle to each guest as a favor.
- **Design welcome baskets** from the winery for each of your guest's hotel rooms. Include a bottle of wine, cheese and crackers, a corkscrew, even T-shirts or tasting books.
- **Go for the gusto:** serve your favorite food and wine combinations. Caviar and champagne; foie gras and sauternes; port and cheese.
- **Serve special sweet wines** with your wedding cake or petits fours, or offer unusual Italian *grappe* or cordials and cognacs after dinner.
- **Order a case of wine to be delivered** to the members of your wedding party while you're on your honeymoon, or sign them up for the winery's wine-of-the-month club. (Be sure to include a note of thanks with the gift.)

bot

Logistics: **MODERATE** | Décor: **SIMPLE** | Personalizing: **MODERATE**

anic garden

Everywhere you look, colorful
blossoms smile on your celebration
as you and your guests stroll a flower-
bedecked path toward cocktails
served on a terrace framed by
moss-covered trees. You marvel, all
your senses tickled—it seems that
this landscape was lovingly sculpted
by the season just for the two of you.

What variety of garden bride
and groom are you? English country,
with its fullness, rich fragrance,
and variety of colors? Asian Zen, with

still pools of water lilies, bamboo, and beautiful grasses? Or perhaps you prefer rare orchids and exotic trees under greenhouse glass. Whatever your style, one thing is certain about any couple who chooses to celebrate in a garden—they love color, texture, and the natural world.

The beauty of choosing a botanic garden as a base for your ceremony or reception is that by its very nature, your venue will reflect your wedding season. It's often a park-like place you can visit throughout the year as you celebrate your lives together. And much of your "décor" is included in the price of admission, which can simplify your design needs.

This romantic late-summer wedding was at the New York Botanical Garden. The guest entrance was marked with an iron arch decorated with flowers. Tables set with simple linens and a variety of centerpieces in purple, wound around along a path dotted with salvia, hibiscus, hydrangea, and other seasonal blooms.

Most metropolitan areas are home to at least one beautiful botanic garden. Chances are you already know of one you like, but if not, consult your local chamber of commerce or tourist information department. Then do your research to find out what is possible. Some gardens have on-site facilities for catering and for sit-down luncheons and dinners. Others may be more loosely organized, offering permits for ceremonies, but no facilities for holding a reception.

Don't forget to ask about any regulations or restrictions, and, as with any outdoor situation, have a back-up plan in case of inclement weather.

To find the perfect garden for your ceremony or reception, start by contacting local botanic associations. Your parks department can also be of service—even in New York City, there is a wonderful array of parks where you can exchange vows at little or no cost, provided you have the appropriate permits in order.

If you'll celebrate in a formal botanic garden, there are lots of things to know. At some gardens outdoor wedding ceremonies and cocktail hours are permitted outside. But décor is limited to things which can be quickly set up and removed without anchoring into the lawn; music is restricted; available times are governed by public hours.

Once you have a garden in mind, you must find out about fees as well as regulations and requirements concerning décor, party hours and set-up times, exclusive or preferred caterers, and so on. Botanic gardens are highly regulated and controlled for good reason—delicate plant species require vigilant care to protect them from trampling and outside contaminants and pests.

Formal gardens offer different options at different times of the year. Flowering trees and shrubs such as dogwood, cherry, and lilac are stunning in the spring months. Rose gardens are generally in bloom from early to mid-summer, and often have additional bloomings in September. Lily pond gardens are often at their best in the later summer months. And perennial gardens, with their dahlias,

GARDEN VARIETY
inspiration

COLORS: Let the season inspire you—late spring offers soft purples, yellows, blues, pastel pinks. Summer provides hotter hues like fuchsia and orange, while fall calls for deep flames and muted reds and coppers. Another year-round favorite—greens in all tones, from viburnum to fern and moss.

FLOWERS: Anything in season and in keeping with your garden of choice—sweet peas, tulips, and flowering branches for spring; hydrangea, peonies, and water lilies or sunflowers for summer; dahlias for early fall, and fiery branches as the season turns.

MATERIALS: Garden urns, flower pots, stone, terra-cotta, ceramic, plants.

HOW IT FEELS: Blowsy, bountiful, seasonal, natural, sensual, fragrant, dreamy.

hibiscus, and salvia, are the showy favorites of late summer through mid-autumn. Ask your garden representative what will be best for your time of year and plan accordingly. But keep in mind that Mother Nature might not always cooperate with your wedding schedule. Inquire about options in the case of a late spring or an early frost.

Let your garden inspire your whole celebration. Ask the contact person about colors and flower varieties for your season, do a little research, and you'll soon have a party that is in perfect harmony both with nature and your own style.

these bouquets of pale purple "Allure" roses are personalized, each with its own collar of fragrant herbs, such as scented geranium, sage, and lavender (above). Guests mingle about the gardens during cocktail hour, sipping lavender-infused rose wine spritzers, amid columns and tables adorned with masses of just one flower: purple hydrangea (opposite).

o allow the colorful garden to take center stage, we kept table details very simple, with white cotton tablecloths, lavender napkins, and white chairs. Rented plates with a delicate floral pattern and cut crystal stemware (also from a rental company) pick up the light.

Exchange vows under a rose-covered arbor or near a majestic willow tree—or in a fragrance garden, with its magical aromas. Incorporate herbs, fragrant cocktail mixers, and edible blossoms into your wedding design. For a special touch, choose a motif for your printed materials which incorporates a peony, lavender sprig, or autumn leaf. Wrap napkins with aromatic rosemary, or use lemon-thyme to flavor your lemonade.

A garden setting often accommodates more colors and textures than I would normally recommend. But a riot of unexpected color in nature somehow works much more successfully than a contrived flower arrangement of scattered, multicolored design. To make the most of this serendipity, I suggest keeping your table décor very simple, with basic linens in limited colors. This way, you'll allow the blooming natural backdrop the glory it deserves. Solid colors, or appropriate floral or botanical prints, are great accents for tablecloths, napkins, and printed items such as place cards and menus.

know your setting

- **Botanic gardens are often charitable** organizations with widely varying rules, regulations, and organizational structures. Some are privately owned, while others are run by local governmental institutions. If you're planning both a ceremony and reception, make sure your garden is well-suited to both. Ask for brochures, a tour of possible sites, recommended caterers and a list of regulations. (Asking for a reference or two from couples who have been married on-site isn't a bad idea, either.)
- **Gardens are generally public spaces** with specific opening hours. This might mean the public could be a part of your ceremony, or that your party cannot begin until an hour when the garden has been officially closed. Find out.
- **Like museums and other public institutions,** gardens often have security guards, parking attendants, and other employees who may need to be compensated for overtime if your party requires it. These extra costs should be outlined in writing to save on confusion later.
- **Some gardens are free;** some require written permits and might require a donation to the garden to gain use of the space. This may or may not be included in the catering fees you'll incur for the party.
- **Many gardens** and other cultural institutions will only allow certain preferred caterers, florists, bands, or other service providers to work on the property. If this is the case, ask for a list of these vendors before committing to the venue, and consult with the vendors so you can be sure you'll be able to work with them.

keep it simple and stunning

- **Stay seasonal.** Although this is a good rule of thumb for any wedding, it is especially important in a garden setting, where the cycle of nature is in full view.
- **Arrange potted plants,** rather than cut flowers as centerpieces and accent décor. One gorgeous flowering azalea or hydrangea is a fraction of the cost of a cut flower design, and makes a very showy presentation. It also makes a lasting

each table is named after a flower, with centerpieces to match (above). An antique garden cart displays "escort posies," small bundles of each table's flowers in pearlized pots, hand-lettered in waterproof ink by twentyandseven, with the guests' names and names of their tables (opposite).

gift for your guests. Just be sure to ask if this is okay with the garden, as some have regulations about bringing in outside plant materials.

- **Don't over-decorate.** Most formal gardens have restrictions against putting lantern or huppah stakes in the ground, or tossing petals or birdseed. Position your garden chairs to face a beautiful spot, and mark the space where you'll exchange vows with two small seedling trees, a hand-carried huppa or an open circle of colorful plants. Add a flower girl carrying a sweet posy and you with your bouquet—and voilà!

- **Organize a short garden tour** for your guests before the ceremony or cocktails, so they'll have a chance to enjoy the beauty of your garden up-close.

- **Create table centerpieces** celebrating the symbolic meaning of plants. (The "Lavender Table" for devotion, the "Rosemary Table" for remembrance, etc.)

- **Instead of a traditional wedding cake,** serve cupcakes adorned with sugar wildflowers. If you'll have a tiered cake, sprinkle edible flower petals atop the layers and serve a petal or two as a garnish with each slice.

- **If you'll have a view of the outside** (and if it is permitted), use inexpensive garden lanterns on stakes to illuminate a path or a seating area where guests might enjoy a fragrant patch of the garden.

- **Use floral or herbal ingredients** in your refreshments. Lemon-verbena lemonade? Orange-flower Bellinis?

W hat could be simpler than this fruit-filled cake with fondant icing (above, left), baked by Elisa Strauss? We added a scattering of fresh, edible rose petals and served each slice with raspberry sauce and a petal or two (page 91). Edible flowers can be included in your wedding menu—these are goat-cheese-stuffed zucchini blossoms, with honey and lavender (above, right).

- **Celebrate your favorite flower in its full glory:** ask your florist to find five varieties of pink rose or tulip, from pale to vibrant, maybe adding a two-toned choice as well. Alternate the shades and styles on your tables for a striking "variation on a theme."

- **Incorporate garden-inspired quotes** or readings into your ceremony and printed materials.

where to splurge

- **Hire a local dance troupe to perform** a May-Day dance for your guests in a corner of the garden.

- **For your centerpieces and guest favors** use rare orchids instead of basic garden plants. Include printed instructions on how to care for these temperamental blooms so family and friends can enjoy them well into the future.

- **Serve a multicourse edible flower-tasting** menu—lotus blossom, lily bulb root, sugared roses, pansy petals, zucchini blossoms. Freeze whole tiny rosebuds in ice cubes or sprinkle fresh herbs and edible nasturtiums or pansies on a simple green salad for a special accent.

- **Have a seamstress sew** hundreds of tiny fresh flowers onto your veil just before the ceremony—and make sure you take lots of pictures!

- **In lieu of favors, donate a tulip bulb** or other flowering plant to the garden in honor of each of your guests. Then make a note in the program to

reality check

- Don't choose a garden for your ceremony if there's no backup indoor or covered space in case of rain. Confusion will certainly occur if you have to change your plans on your wedding day.

- Never bank on nature. You may schedule your ceremony to coincide perfectly with the blooming of the lilac grove or the Cherry Blossom Festival, but sometimes Mother N. just doesn't cooperate. You'll need to either be okay with that, or have an alternate, and equally beautiful, plan.

- Make sure you understand regulations governing your party. Read your contract very carefully to avoid any confusion before, during, or after the celebration. Ask questions early and plan accordingly.

- A note to the bride: spare yourself agony on the big day. Unless they don't mind grass and dirt stains, garden-style brides should avoid trains and wear ankle-length or shorter gowns. I once watched a catering manager scrub the bottom of a garden bride's dress between the ceremony and cocktails—don't let that be you.

- Be aware of any allergies you may have to pollen, bees, or other plants or insects. You wouldn't want a bee sting or a sneeze-inducing fragrance to ruin the most beautiful day of your life.

let them know they'll forever be a part of your wedding garden. Check with your garden in advance regarding donations, as each has differing regulations and programs.

Logistics: **DIFFICULT** | Décor: **MODERATE** | Personalizing: **SIMPLE**

at home

This is the moment you've dreamed
of your whole life. You float
through the doors that lead to the
patio, where your truly near and dear
are gathered under the flower-
blanketed arbor your mother planted
when you were just a child. To your
left is the tree you used to climb,
now adorned with ribbons holding
magical wind chime gifts for
your guests. Straight ahead is your
future, filled with promise. And all
around you is home, sweet home.

intimate informality

For some brides and grooms, there is just no place like home when it comes to hosting their perfect wedding celebration. Often it is the bride's or groom's family home, a place she or he grew up in and holds dear. Sometimes it is a country house where happy summers or festive winters were spent with loved ones. A home-style wedding can also be hosted at the home or apartment of a beloved friend or family member, or even at the couple's residence.

this breezy at-home ceremony is set under a lush green arbor, with mixed garden and ice-cream store chairs, and a pair of azalea topiaries on painted plant stands. Lengths of diaphanous pink muslin tied to the top of the arbor create a backdrop for the vow space and soften the view of nearby houses.

I love to see a couple at home on their wedding day, the bride dressing in the room where she slept as a girl, the groom playing with his dogs on the front lawn or relaxing by the pool with newspaper and coffee. There is a continuum of memory and tradition that is deeply layered when special moments are celebrated at home.

If home is where you'd like to tie the knot, you must first consider the size of your guest list. If you're lucky, perhaps you have a giant penthouse apartment with a terrace or dining room large enough to accommodate 50 guests for the ceremony or even for a sit-down feast. More likely you're working with a smaller, more intimate setting which requires more planning and calls for a more casual approach.

The number of guests which constitutes a small, intimate backyard wedding is governed by the number of people you could comfortably fit inside your home should you need to. You would have to be able to fit tables or seating for everyone, plus facilities to accommodate their needs, such as a place to hang coats, and adequate bathroom facilities, inside your home.

Any guest count which stretches these criteria makes me utter four utterly un-simple words: "Call the tent company." If you're hosting an at-home wedding larger than your home can accommodate, See the Tent chapter for more information on what's involved. If, on the other hand, you prefer a small, casual party, or if you will be hosting any part of your celebration—such as a shower or post-wedding brunch—at home, you may find this chapter helpful.

Chances are you've hosted a party at home before. Just keep in mind that you'll need to provide bathroom facilities, shelter, and seating for everyone. Ask neighbors to lend you old picnic tables and benches or chairs. (While you're at it, make sure to invite them, or at least let them know about the wedding so you won't encounter any complaints on the day of the party.)

AT-HOME
inspiration

COLORS: What suits your home? Sunny yellows, happy plaids, natural greens, bridal whites? Celebrate the styles and colors all around you.

FLOWERS: Casual blossoms from the garden—daisies, sunflowers, tulips, hydrangeas, garden roses.

MATERIALS: Flea-market finds, mix-and-match tables, chairs and tableware, buckets and baskets, flowerpots.

HOW IT FEELS: Personal, intimate, casual, fun, familial, heirloom.

CROSS-REFERENCE: The Country Inn, Loft, and Tent chapters are good places to look for more advice.

Consider your hosts as well. If the wedding is not at your own home, make sure to include the homeowner in all important decisions, and always ask permission for elements like live music, additional power sources, and décor installation. (They might not want your florist staple-gunning garland around their front door.) By the same token, if there is something special your host would like to highlight—a favorite flower, or a particular collection of paintings—try to incorporate it somehow if possible.

Remember that at a home wedding, all of the basic elements which would normally be provided by a rental venue must be taken care of by you. This

he words "love, sweet love" appear on various details, from a welcome wreath (page 102) to these clothespin paperweights, which secured personal notes to each guest from the bride and groom (above). Borrowed wooden tables are scattered on the lawn, decorated with cotton runners and mix-and-match leftover vases used as candleholders. A few flowers, in bud vases, were plucked from a local market (opposite).

means provisions for garbage disposal, septic maintenance, even hand towels and extra toilet tissue for the bathrooms, must all be arranged by you. You'll have to gather or rent plates, silverware, chairs, glasses, and tablecloths. And unless you hire a caterer, you and your family or friends will be responsible for all the cooking and cleaning up.

If your wedding will take place or continue after sunset, you must also consider appropriate outdoor lighting—and unless you're in an enclosed patio, you'll want to provide insect repellent or citronella candles to help keep bugs away.

Serve foods from a hutch or sideboard (opposite, above). Borrowed or flea market-purchased plates and platters create a more eclectic look. Hutch drawers can be filled with silverware and napkins. Punch or sangria stays bug-free when served from covered jars. We arranged glasses in a wire basket and offered frozen watermelon chunks instead of ice cubes (opposite, below).

Your home or the home of a friend or relative may be perfect for your rehearsal dinner or wedding shower. The point is to keep it easy and relaxed. Do make sure to arrange for parking if your driveway or street won't accommodate enough cars. And if you do host your wedding at home, think about reserving a suite at a local inn or hotel where you can be whisked away for the wedding night.

What I don't suggest is that you do it all yourself. You must create your own wedding style, but not necessarily your own bridal bouquets, centerpieces, and entrees. Just because you're holding your wedding at home, you are not obliged to provide homemade everything. Decide what you want your level of involvement to be as far as preparation, setup, and service, and then make plans that suit your budget, your wishes, and your time.

know your setting

- **Figure out your maximum guest count** and determine if your location will accommodate that number comfortably. Consider calling in a tent professional for a consultation to determine your maximum capacity indoors and your options for adding a tent structure should your guest list grow. Most tent companies provide complimentary consultations.

- **If you will require extra power** for live music or lighting, have a professional evaluate your needs and make recommendations. You wouldn't want to blow a fuse in the middle of your wedding.

- **If the home is not your own,** have a pre-planning meeting with your host, or with each other if you'll hold the wedding in your own nest. Review preferences and priorities to make sure everyone is "on the same page."

- **Check local regulations regarding live music,** assembly, and garbage disposal. Call your local town or village administrator and ask for a list of any regulations.

keep it simple and stunning

- **Decorate your home.** Adorn the entrance gate or front door with a welcome wreath, or add a garland to the patio. Personalize it with photos of both of your families. If guests will be inside the house, place small vases of flowers on coffee tables and in bathrooms.

- **Consider borrowing furniture** and accessories. An at-home wedding is the perfect setting for an eclectic mix of tables, chairs, plates, silver, and glasses. Just be aware that if you borrow elements, you're responsible for any damage and for coordinating both pick-up and the timely, safe return of these items.

- **Or rent items.** It's certainly easier to call a rental company for tables and chairs, and even plates and glasses if necessary than to scramble around looking for them. Many rental companies have casual garden chairs and benches that make for a great look and a homey feel. Rentals might cost more than borrowing, but they're convenient. They'll be delivered to your door and picked up again; and you don't even have to wash the dishes—the company takes care of all that.

- **Move precious objects and clutter** out of the way. This way, you and your hosts won't have to worry about accidental breakage, and guests will have more room to move about freely. Take up

I f you'll have little ones attending, make them feel special: provide a basket of toys or games. For one at-home wedding I designed, the bride prepared small gifts for each child, and we placed the gifts in a small basket hung from a low branch of a kid-friendly tree. You can do the same with candy favors and a sign like this one.

any delicate carpets that might be damaged and make arrangements for dirty shoes in the case of wet weather. If your wedding will be all indoors, you could consider providing slippers for your guests, like the Japanese do.

● **Preparing for and cleaning up** after a wedding is a big task. You might want to hire a professional cleaning service to help with pre- and post-wedding tidying. Check with your hosts to see if there's a service they prefer, and make sure you take care of the bill if the home is not your own.

● **Inform or invite your neighbors.** Bring them a basket of baked goods or a bottle of wine and let them know what's happening. Chances are they'll be congratulatory and accommodating. If not, at least you know what to expect, so you can be prepared.

● **If you'll be providing all** the beverages and food, call on a local restaurateur or friend in the catering business to help you with a list of what you should have on hand. I always recommend limiting choices and making sure to have plenty of those items (you can always use them for your next party!). For the bar, beer and wine, along with plenty of sodas, punch, and water, lemons, and limes, is fine. If you want more options, add one type of each of the major liquors—vodka, gin, and whisky—along with juices, tonic, and seltzer. Avoid complicated or obscure mix-in ingredients. Your guests will understand.

● **Host a Sweet Southern Barbecue,** with pulled pork, ribs and chicken, and microbrewed beer tucked into ice-filled crates or buckets. Give away bottles of hot sauce as favors and hire a small country music ensemble to provide down-home music. Or make an Heirloom Potluck Party, with each guest assigned to bring a favorite family recipe (and recipe card for your cookbook). Use paper plates, or gather mix-and-match china from grandma's attic and mom's cabinets, and use everything all together for an eclectic, vintage feel.

where to splurge

- **Hire a fantastic local chef** or caterer and set up one long, immaculately dressed table filled with all your favorite foods. Voilà—a moveable feast in your own backyard!

- **Enhance your landscape.** Have a garden specialist look at your property and make suggestions for additional plantings appropriate to the season. Build a "wedding arbor"—this beautiful space will grow and thrive in the years to come as a special reminder of your celebration.

- **Commission an artist** to make a drawing or engraving of your home. Use this as a graphic image on all your printed materials—invitations, thank-you cards, etc. Then give the engraving to your host, or if the wedding is at your own home, hang the artwork in a special place.

- **Hire the local school marching band** to play your favorite song just after the ceremony.

reality check

▥ Just because you're getting married at home, you don't necessarily have to do everything yourself. A florist can use your vases and provide bouquets for your bridesmaids and you. A few freelance waiters and a bartender can make a huge difference in the smooth flow of your party. An experienced caterer can take all the pressure off you and your hosts, whether it's a casual clambake or a serious sit-down meal.

▥ Inquire about additional insurance. There are a number of ways to add to your homeowner's policy to protect you and your guests. Call your broker or insurance company and ask what will work best for you.

▥ Have plenty of supplies on hand. Paper goods such as toilet tissue and paper towels, first-aid supplies, and insect repellent are especially important.

▥ Do not assume you'll be able to rent a tent at the last minute. Tents are reserved far in advance and municipal permits and planning are required. Decide right away whether you want to have a tent, so there will be no surprises. (See the Tent chapter for more information.)

▥ Most damage to your home and property is avoidable, but some should be expected. Accidents happen anywhere large numbers of people gather. Lawn damage and broken household items top the list, along with scratched or scraped walls, and stained furniture. Move valuable objects out of the way and allow plenty of space for your guests to mingle. Discuss how you'll deal with any damages in advance with each other and your hosts.

museu

Logistics: **DIFFICULT** | Décor: **SIMPLE** | Personalizing: **SIMPLE**

m or gallery

You've always wanted to have
dinner with your favorite artist.
Now every aspect of your
wedding celebration is surrounded
by beauty, and infused with
creativity, color, and inspiration.
Each detail is an opportunity to
think out-of-the box. Family
and friends agree—this is a truly
unique party they'll never forget.

the art of celebrating

A museum or gallery wedding can be modern or classical, avant-garde or uber-elegant. After all, museums and galleries are home to every imaginable object, from every time period. Sculptures, paintings, drawings, architectural renderings and historical arti-facts—there are museums and galleries to showcase all of these. More and more, art-related venues are permitting weddings and other events to take place in their spaces on a regular basis.

New York City's Chelsea Art Museum was the backdrop for this celebration. Inspired by the painting of artist Jean Miotte, we looked for ways to create details and décor which were creative and unusual, like submerging this single giant stem of heliconia upside down.

If you're an art-loving couple, you'll probably want to celebrate in a setting which features an artist or medium you enjoy. Or perhaps you just love the architecture of a particular museum. Either way, there is a wide range of options to explore, especially in urban areas. Museums and galleries are housed in former factories, warehouse spaces, historic build-ings, old mansions—you name it. You must simply find the one that's right for you.

Start by exploring the museums or galleries you know and love. Make an appointment with the staff to discuss possibilities and decide your guest list in advance to be sure the space is appropriate for your party.

An art-filled setting is exactly that, a visually pleasing space which is designed to delight or pro-voke, to inspire and move its visitors. You can have cocktails with Rodin, Cézanne, or Van Gogh, and dinner with Warhol. Or you can view an exhibition of fine glass or high fashion before inviting your guests to a magnificent catered dinner in a beaux-arts court or a rococo rotunda.

What you must know is that many museums, to protect their precious contents, have long lists of restrictions and very stringent guidelines for events held in their spaces. These regulations involve the numbers of guests, party times, catering concerns, and insurance for any damages caused as a result of your celebration.

Look at the architecture of the space you've chosen to tell you what type of flowers to feature and how to arrange them. In this cutting-edge envi-ronment, I thought it would be fun to turn flowers topsy-turvy for our accent pieces. Focus on just one or two types of unusual flowers, and turn them upside-down, or submerge them in clear water. The water enhances the color of the blossoms, and if you use flowers with flexible stems, such as calla lilies or orchids, you can create fluid, unusual arrangements which are both inexpensive and inno-vative. This is a great centerpiece idea as well, and allows you to get away with using a minimal num-ber of blooms for maximal visual effect.

If your museum is more classical in design, take your design cues from the exhibits or the architecture and colors in the space. Be creative and infuse your tabletop, party favors, invitations and programs with drawings, monograms, or even quotes from your favorite artists.

know your setting

- **Museums are a lot like botanic gardens** in terms of their regulations—their staff members have to protect the artwork from damage and theft while still hosting events which bring in income, as well as interest and support for their collections. Insist on a written list of regulations before you decide to book your wedding, and make sure you're comfortable with all the details.

- **Because museums and galleries are open** to the public, your party time may be restricted to days or hours when the museum is closed. Find out if you'll have adequate set up and breakdown time, and inquire about overtime arrangements and charges.

- **Museums and galleries change** their exhibitions throughout the year. I once planned a wedding around three large paintings which had always been in the gallery. The week of the wedding they were removed to accommodate another exhibition. Be sure you know what will be hanging or displayed at the time of your wedding.

ARTISTIC
inspiration

COLORS: If there is a lot of color in the artwork, keep your palette simple and understated. In a more neutral space, you can punch up your accents with bold color or geometric prints.

FLOWERS: In an impressionist or classical setting, use garden-style or blowsy flowers like those you'd see in a Renoir or Monet. In more abstract settings, choose dramatic orchids, heliconia, giant green leaves, protea, twisted horsetail bamboo, or other unusual elements.

MATERIALS: Glass, ceramic, leather, stone, metal, plastic, festive papers.

HOW IT FEELS: Different, inspirational, creative, cool, interesting.

CROSS-REFERENCE: The Loft and Botanic Garden chapters are good places to look for more ideas, as well as the Hotel chapter if lighting design is appropriate.

These serpentine tables are draped with custom white faux leather tablecloths, created by Linda Lieberman for Just Linens. (This concept could be created less expensively in cotton.) Clustered glass vases hold two Italian poppies, each in bold colors that "pop" against Jean Miotte's artwork. Store-bought zebra-print note cards became place cards, with the guests' names printed on white paper and then glued to the front. The modern plates and glasses were rentals.

his hand-wired bouquet of just one type of flower—cattleya orchids—is accented with a collar of lush yellow ostrich feathers (above). To jazz up basic white ballroom chairs, we had less expensive "shirt back" chair covers sewn in faux leather to match the tablecloths, then pinned a single fresh poppy to each, right before the party (opposite).

- **On that same note,** be aware of the content of any exhibitions which might be on display during your event. If you or your guests have problems with nudity or disturbing images, you'll want to know about them in advance.

- **For security reasons,** some museums and galleries prohibit or restrict photography and videography. Inquire about policies regarding photography in your space.

keep it simple and stunning

- **Let the artwork inspire you.** Quote Picasso on your menu. Name cocktails after your featured artist. If you'll celebrate in front of a painting of sunflowers, decorate the whole space with these happy blossoms.

- **Don't be afraid of unusual materials.** Colorful glass, rare flowers, interesting fabrics—this is your chance to be different.

- **Create an "art station" for your guest book.** Have an instant camera on hand, along with glue, markers, and other fun components, and encourage your guests to write a poem, take a photo, or just "be creative." Make sure to check with your venue regarding any regulations for pens, markers, or other restricted materials.

- **Serve from buffets that are coordinated** with your environment. A Monet Garden Buffet or a

Ron Ben-Israel created this whimsical cake, decked out with sugar poppies, to match our theme (above). Stephen Kennard and Diane Grinnell of Canard Caterers created a specialty Indonesian Rice Table buffet for cocktail hour. We used inexpensive take-out containers as bowls, and offered a variety of vegetarian and meat-based dishes to top the rice (opposite).

Ming Dynasty Station are wonderful alternatives to traditional carving tables and crudités. Invite your caterer to join in the creative process.

- **Design a painted cake.** Instead of expensive sugar flowers, ask your baker to make a sugar "painting" on your cake in the style of your artistic surroundings or featured artist. Water lilies, cubist shapes, floating cherubs, minimalist geometry—send your baker postcards or links to your artist's website for inspiration.

- **Instead of fancy favors,** make a donation to the museum in the name of your guests. Include a note on their place card, menu, or program to let them know you've done so.

- **If you're hosting your ceremony at a museum,** you might not have a "bride's room" or a place to get ready. If so, make other arrangements—it's your wedding day, after all!

where to splurge

- **Commission a painting** for your new home from one of the gallery's artists and have it unveiled at the rehearsal dinner or wedding.

- **Arrange a private viewing** of a favorite exhibition for your guests during the party.

- **Give books of the artist's work** to your guests as favors.

- **Hire a portrait artist** to make sketches of your guests or your wedding party.

reality check

- Candles are not always permitted in museums and galleries, and sometimes there are special flame-retardant requirments for fabrics brought into a museum setting.

- Some galleries and museums have labyrinthine, but connected, spaces which are used for larger parties. Make sure you're happy with the floor plan for your highest possible number of guests so you won't feel the party is split up into too many rooms.

- You might be limited to specific, pre-approved caterers, photographers, musicians, or other service providers. Ask for a list and check references before you decide to hold your wedding in the space.

- Although I always recommend that couples obtain copies of vendor insurance certificates at a wedding where artwork is involved in this setting, I really think it's an absolute must.

- If your museum ceremony will be a religious one, make sure your officiant won't object to any symbols or sculptures in the space. I once designed a wedding where the officiant insisted that we cover bas-relief nude sculptures of Olympic athletes during the ceremony. Don't let this happen to you!

Caterers often have special serving pieces on hand to liven up your party, so make sure to inquire. Canard set up these pyramids of stacking Lucite in front of one of the museum's circular paintings to create an architectural display of colorful cocktails named after the couple's favorite artists.

sta

Logistics: **SIMPLE** | Décor: **DIFFICULT** | Personalizing: **MODERATE**

ndard hotel

Room for everyone who wants to stay. Amenities and services for you and your guests. Plenty of space for your ceremony and reception. Professional staff to coordinate the big day, and a convenient location to boot. Add a few special details to make this space your own and you'll have the best of both simplicity and convenience for your wedding.

just add light and magic

Like many other types of venues, hotels come in all shapes and sizes, from ranch-style spa destinations to chandelier-bedecked, white-glove havens of rococo-ceilinged ballrooms. Hotels are by nature places of great hospitality, designed to host people for the night, the weekend, or longer. If you've chosen a hotel replete with architectural detail, whether modern or historic, you'll want to embrace that style and let it inspire your whole celebration.

I design many weddings in hotel settings, and a number of these hotels tend to be formal in style and already highly decorated, with fine silver and china and a staff waiting to serve your every need or whim. These weddings are some of the easiest to design and plan, as the hotels offer tables, chairs, a planning staff, chefs, linens, and many other amenities to make your experience special and pleasant. I design in such a way as to complement their specific architecture and I work with the couple to personalize with details that coordinate—beaded tablecloths to match chandeliers, fine stationery with the hotel crest for menus and place cards, formal ball gowns for the bride and her attendants.

What is much more common, however, is the hotel wedding in a multi-use facility—a hotel which hosts just as many (or more) corporate and business events as it does weddings or social fêtes. While the services at these hotels are often just as fantastic as fancier hotel locations, the décor tends to be more neutral, with a less romantic palette and design scheme—a sort of muted blank slate for any kind of gathering. These hotels are much more common than those of a landmark or high-design bent. So that's the type of hotel wedding I have chosen to discuss in this chapter.

Of course, all hotels host both business and personal functions—some are just more architecturally moderate or nondescript, leaving the spirit of each event to fill in the ambiance. If you'll be married in this kind of hotel, you'll want to focus on personalizing your celebration in as many ways as possible. Whereas a country inn or restaurant wedding offers instant personality, a wedding in a corporate hotel cries out for you to infuse it with your own personal touches.

This chapter is the perfect place to talk about two of the most important elements in wedding design—lighting and linens. It is my belief that, across the board, lighting is the single most important factor in creating mood for a celebration. When used artistically, light can literally work magic—think of

The Sheraton Meadowlands Hotel in New Jersey is the perfect backdrop for demonstrating the power of good lighting (opposite, above). Here is one of the hotel's multi-function rooms in its normal state. Throughout this chapter, all the larger room shots are taken from this same angle. Lighting designer Ken Lapham of Eventlights brought in fixtures to create multiple moods (opposite, below).

the difference between a fluorescent-lit office and a candlelit restaurant. And because the normal lighting in a corporate or multi-use hotel is so unmagical, it is one place where I strongly recommend engaging the help of a professional lighting designer.

The beauty and power of light is that it can highlight what you desire to draw attention to, and hide, or draw attention away from, elements that are undesirable or unattractive. I'm fond of saying that the right light level is the best gift you can give your guests, because it makes everyone look and feel better.

One of my favorite lighting stories involves a lovely couple who were both very creative—the groom was an architect, the bride an art teacher. They were to be married in an historic building, on a park-like property in the Chelsea neighborhood of Manhattan. When we began working together, I suggested the idea of lighting design, but the couple was adamant that they didn't want their wedding to feel like a Broadway show. I suggested we visit the site together to discuss various possibilities. It was then we discovered that none of the lights in the space were dimmable—in other words, the lights had two options: on or off. In addition, there was no accent lighting shining on any of the fantastic gothic architectural details in the space.

Despite these discoveries, this elegant bride and groom were still reluctant to spend money on lighting. It didn't help that we were standing in the space in the middle of the day, which made it hard to imagine what it would look like during the evening party.

I asked the couple to do me a favor before they made a final decision. "Just stop by here one evening at around the time of your reception," I said. "Walk in, take a look around, then call me and tell me you are comfortable with that level of light for your wedding night."

Suffice it to say I got a call the same evening—they had done what I asked and seen what I meant! We brought a professional in to light the celebration and it was truly one of the most magical transformations of a space I've ever seen. And there wasn't anything even remotely "Broadway" about it. What many people don't understand is that you can create almost any effect with lighting. In this case, I called our design "enhanced candlelight:" and, using soft ambers and clear lights, our design team made the room seem as if it were entirely lit by glowing candles, the way it might have been when it was first built.

On page 127 there is a "before" photo of the ballroom; all of the photographs here are taken from exactly the same angle. In the "before" shot, you can see that there's really nothing at all wrong with the space—it's what you would expect from a high-quality, standard hotel. But the photos that feature variations on lighting and linens illustrate the visual punch you can get from imaginative use of color and texture in your lighting plan.

Many brides and grooms ask me about using candlelight. "Won't it be enough if we just add candles in the center of the table?" My answer is that candlelight helps a lot and is one of my favorite decorative elements. In some cases it's perfect and the

COLORS: If your space is neutral, you can transform it with color, pop pinks and reds, soft ambers, romantic lavenders—use linen and lighting to reinforce color.

FLOWERS: The options are endless—classic calla lilies, modern orchids, soft hydrangeas—decide what your overall look will be and choose accordingly.

MATERIALS: Glass, silver, ceramic, fine linens, monograms, lighting.

HOW IT FEELS: Flexible, easy, convenient, service-oriented, one-stop.

CROSS-REFERENCE: See the Loft and Museum chapters for more modern spaces. The Private Club chapter offers great advice for more traditional weddings.

only appropriate choice (such as on the beach or in a restaurant). And if you can't afford or don't have access to professional lighting design, then that's your best solution.

Yet, if you look across a large room which is purely candlelit, depending upon the setting, you can sometimes end up with a sort of monotonous general light quality, in which the level that the candlelit glow is at is very pretty, but the overall feeling in the room above and below that level can be a bit dull. If you really need to transform a space, you'll want targeted, focused lighting in key areas, coordinated with the rest of your overall design.

ook at the chairs in your hotel ballroom. We replaced darker chairs with a more bridal white ballroom-style chair, and added romance with a single blossom of lavender hydrangea (at live). This ceremony was set in a corner to create depth and interest with the lighting. Organic light stencils and soft lavender tones soften and add an ethereal quality to an otherwise nondescript space (opposite).

When you visit a hotel space, or any other space for that matter, inquire about lighting. Can you bring perimeter lights up while keeping central chandeliers lower? Is the cost of pin-spotting your tables (pointing a single, clear light at the center of the table) included with your wedding package? If not, is there a reputable lighting design company the hotel can recommend for you?

know your setting

My colleague, Ken Lapham, lighting designer, has a few pieces of good advice for couples considering lighting design in their wedding spaces.

First, make sure you're dealing with a professional. Ken suggests asking your hotel for recommendations, or consulting with a local theater company. Note: Don't forget to check insurance certificates and references for any vendors you're considering.

Next, ask your designer to coordinate with the hotel or venue, and find out in advance if power requirements will be an issue. Profes-

sional lighting often requires extra power and can result in extra charges to bring in lines or generators where necessary.

Inquire in advance about union requirements. Many venues require the use of union labor, which can be a factor in both the cost and the execution of your designs. A reputable designer should be able to take care of these details for you.

Check your ceiling height: not every room is a great candidate for lighting design. Ken recommends a ceiling height of at least 12 feet so lights won't shine in your guests' eyes.

the beauty of fine linen

You can see from the photos in this book how a very colorful or beautifully textured fabric can transform a room. Most hotels and many other locations offer basic white or ivory tablecloths and corporate style chairs. You'll want to look at your options before deciding what's important to you.

It's often hard to tell from a small swatch how linen can add decorative punch and magic to a space. But trust me on this: if you have ten or twenty tables, all decked with a bright color or a beautiful fabric, there is a dramatic effect across the entire room. Keep in mind that you don't need the most expensive fabrics to make a visual statement—bold colors or ethereal patterns on simple organza overlays may be all you need.

this magical space is the same corner pictured on page 127. We simply changed the chairs, and added Ken's soft, textured lighting and tablecloths. Simple cotton undercloths are topped with shimmering sheer overlays. Candle centerpieces are arranged in low, water-filled bowls with white pillar candles, surrounded by clear votives.

know your setting

- **From a planning standpoint,** hotels are generally very easy venues. Many have planning offices with a full staff dedicated to events and banquets. Use these experts as your guides in creating floor plans, menus that work well, even transportation arrangements for your guests.

- **Like many other venues,** hotels often have lists of preferred vendors, which may mean extra charges or permissions if you wish to bring in an outside florist. They may require insurance certificates and other clearances, so make sure to secure a list of requirements and restrictions before booking nonpreferred vendors.

- **When you're hosting a wedding at a hotel,** it is often possible to negotiate a discounted rate for blocks of rooms for your guests and wedding party. Ask about special packages and discounts and be sure to check any cancellation policies or deposit requirements.

Once again, lighting and linens serve to transform the room into a completely different space—this time a spicy, sexy celebration in red and pink. Vivid geometric gobos are projected onto the walls, and the more ethereal tablecloths of the previous pages are replaced with simple, solid red cotton.

- **Hotels often have multiple events in progress** at the same time. Make sure you know what's planned for your wedding day—another wedding, perhaps? If so, review timing and parking and space arrangements to insure your guests won't be confused or delayed by other revelers.

- **Ask to meet your day-of-event staff.** Remember that your banquet planner may not be on-site on your wedding day, so you'll want to make a positive connection with the team who will be in charge on the day of the party.

keep it simple and stunning

- **Personalize the space.** One great idea is to create a welcome table with photos of the two of you as children or as a couple, or wedding photos from both of your families.

- **Check the size of your chairs.** Remember that many standard rental chair covers do not fit on hotel chairs, which are often larger or irregularly shaped.

- **Focus on lighting instead** of giant flower arrangements—the right light is the most powerful tool for creating mood in a neutral space.

- **Point a single, clear light** at the center of each dining table (designers call this "pin-spotting"), and accent plain walls and floors with color washes or light stencils (known as "gobos").

We've layered red throughout the party, with details like red amaryllis centerpieces, striped place cards, and red glass votives (above, left). Personalize a more "corporate" space by bringing yourselves into it. A welcome table with a few personal photos is a great idea, as is a guest book for warm wishes on this special day (above, right).

- **Coordinate your cake** with your colors, flowers, or theme. If the hotel baker will create your cake, send swatches or a sketch to help inspire the design.
- **Rent or purchase fine linens.** This is a great way to personalize your wedding with both color and texture.
- **Ask about the use of extra spaces.** One bride I know didn't want to have to use the same ballroom for her ceremony and dinner; she was concerned about transition times and creating chaos that her guests might witness. She inquired about a separate ballroom on a whim and was granted the use of the extra space at no charge. This gave us plenty of time for setup. It never hurts to ask!
- **Place any large flower arrangements** at key focal points, such as an entrance or in an architectural alcove, rather than on random pedestals or in corners.

where to splurge

- **Have a champagne fountain** at cocktail hour.
- **Replace corporate chairs** with rented ballroom chairs and custom covers.
- **Create a lounge space** in one corner of the room or in an adjoining space. Give it a theme, such as a Moroccan lounge or a Blue Zen Den, and coordinate lighting, music, after dinner drinks, and snacks for your guests.

reality check

- Some hotels have union labor requirements. This may mean that only certain authorized tasks can be performed by the staff, and that they might not be permitted to perform other tasks, such as lighting candles provided by an outside vendor (like your florist). Find out what the rules are and ask your vendors to coordinate with the banquet office in case extra vendor staff will have to remain on hand.

- Know your party times. Many hotels have specific windows of time which you purchase when hosting a party. Make sure you'll have adequate time for vendors to set up and decorate each of your spaces, that there is a plan if the party should continue late; and that you have any information you need if vendors must return to remove ceremony elements, props, containers, linens, etc. Request a list of all these times in writing. Remember that overtime charges may apply for both labor and space rental costs.

- Many hotels require photo identification from vendors entering the building for security reasons—find out what the rules are, and let your vendors know what's required.

- **Take an extra suite** in the hotel for an after-party.
- **Invite your bridal party** to arrive a day early and treat them to breakfast in bed as a great start to the wedding day.

Logistics: **DIFFICULT** | Décor: **MODERATE** | Personalizing: **SIMPLE**

loft

A hip address on your invitations.
Light streaming through giant
windows that look out across the
city. An open space to make
your own. Serene or spicy, cool
or colorful, warehouse, studio,
penthouse or former factory—the
loft is an eager blank canvas
waiting to be transformed by your
unique artistic wedding vision.

offbeat
elegance

If you're considering a loft space for your wedding, you're probably a bit artistic, design-oriented, and perhaps a little informal in your everyday approach. You want to celebrate your wedding in a space that is flexible, open, and unique. You might also like the fact that because most lofts are located in commercial buildings, you don't have to worry if the party goes late or becomes loud.

Many urban areas and restored industrial enclaves have amazing loft spaces with incredible scale and detail that are sometimes less expensive to rent than hotels or restaurants. But a wedding in a loft is almost never a truly simple production, as the space is often an empty, if interesting, shell.

for a less expensive, yet striking, bouquet, consider clustering a mass of simple flowers, such as these rose-like carnations—yes, carnations! Many common flowers, such as alstromeria, gerbera daisies, and tulips, now come in a variety of pretty colors. Ask your florist about your options.

What the loft wedding allows for in terms of creativity, it demands in detailed planning. Consider that every single fork, spoon, chair, napkin, food ingredient and serving dish must be rented, transported, and set up for each new event. The same goes for accent furnishings and decorative fixtures—many lofts are raw spaces without permanent seating, bar, or lounge areas. There are lots of great prop and party rental companies which can help you find all the perfect pieces, but remember that everything you must bring in adds to your décor and delivery budget.

Most wedding-appropriate lofts are commercial spaces, but of course you might choose to celebrate in a residential loft—the home of a friend or relative. In this case, you'll want to consider advice from the At Home chapter as well. You'll also want to carefully investigate any regulations which apply as to music, noise, and other party issues.

The most beautiful loft weddings focus on enhancing, not transforming, the space. Sure, it's possible to turn a converted warehouse into an eighteenth-century ballroom or a sultan's palace, but if your goal is simple beauty (and a reasonable budget), you'll want to concentrate on working with what's there.

Despite the fact that many loft spaces are in old buildings, they often call for a more contemporary and eclectic approach. In general, strong colors and simple geometric prints are best for linens, and fussy flower arrangements should be avoided in favor of masses of just one or two types of blossoms.

If your loft space features white as a prominent color, you might also choose to decorate with a modern, but more bridal, palette of whites, greens, and creams. Consider the overall effect you want to create: soft, ethereal, Zen, and serene? Or spicy, passionate, bold and festive?

White decorative accents in a white space create a
serene, modern feeling, especially when combined
with elegant food presentations (above). For this wedding, caterer
Olivier Cheng created an elegant salmon appetizer. New York
City's Loft Eleven was the setting for the colorful celebration
pictured here and on the cover (opposite). We set square and
rectangular tables with custom coral linens and geometric dinnerware. The centerpieces are ribbon-wrapped glass vases with Latin
Ambience roses and white feathers. Place settings are accented
with personalized paper napkin wraps (page 137) and chopsticks.

LOFTY
inspiration

COLORS: White with accents in hot pink, apple green, orange, mustard, chocolate brown, cranberry, or peacock blue. Or go Zen with naturals and whites.

FLOWERS: Orchids, gloriosa lilies, nerene, tulips, papyrus, calla lilies, poppies, branches, leaves, bamboo, paper-whites, and unusual roses.

MATERIALS: Glass, wood, metal, paper, simple ceramics, pillar, and votive candles.

HOW IT FEELS: Airy, funky, sharp, hip, bold, sexy, cutting-edge, nontraditional, light, open.

CROSS-REFERENCE: The Tent, Hotel, and Museum chapters offer good logistical advice for Loft weddings, and almost any chapter's design story can be implemented here.

baker Colette Peters of Colette's Cakes created this geometric cake to match our wedding colors. Instead of flowers, I gave her a swatch of the fabric from our chair covers (pages 140-141) for inspiration. She combined an architectural design with whimsical, confetti-like accents—evocative of New Year's in New York City.

As lofts are often, square, or rectangular spaces with high ceilings, using geomotry in you table shapes and decorative accents can be a wonderful idea. Square tables are now available from many rental companies, as are rectangular and serpentine shapes. Combining squares and rectangles is a great way to create a modern table configuration. While square tables can limit your seating arrangements (it can be difficult to put odd numbers of guests on one side of a square), adding rectangles allows you to arrange any tables with an odd number of guests without a problem. If you do choose rectangular tables, make sure they're wide enough to accommodate your place settings and decorations. I generally recommend a 48" width (or wider) for tables with centerpieces, and 36" minimum width to allow enough space for two guests to be seated comfortably across from each other.

Whether you choose round or rectangular tables, plan your dinnerware and centerpieces to match in coordinating shapes. There are so many great plates and vases available—squares, circles, low bowls. In a loft setting, it's often possible to be more "arty" and creative with décor, using just a few blooms to dramatic effect. Ask your florist to suggest unusual ideas in keeping with your overall vision.

Many lofts also have couches or other furniture pieces which can be used to accent your wedding celebration. Take advantage of as many as possible to add warmth and style to your welcome table, or in a lounge or cocktail area. Just make sure to find out about any costs for damages in case of

spillage or other accidents. If your colors don't match the furniture design, you can always cover a couch or chair with a piece of coordinating fabric.

An important issue to consider is light, as many lofts have only industrial-style or fluorescent fixtures. If not equipped with dimmable lighting, lofts benefit greatly from the help of a professional lighting designer. Uplights on architectural details, soft pin-spots on your tables and accent lighting for the dance floor area can transform a space. (See the Hotel chapter for more information on lighting design.) Be sure to check with your venue—you might wish to visit the space during an event to look at the light levels available. If you'll use candles, choose basic votives and pillars over more old-fashioned styles, and arrange them in simple patterns.

know your setting

- **Lofts are often multiuse spaces** that are rented out for everything from photo shoots to fashion shows, corporate events and weddings. It can be difficult to envision how the rooms will be set up by just looking at an empty space. Consult your loft representative about previous weddings and party designs to find out about plans that have worked in the space before. Ask to see pictures of the room set up for an event, or if possible, visit the site during setup for an upcoming wedding or party.

- **Some lofts are equipped with kitchens,** refurbished elevators, nice bathrooms, and other amenities, but others are not. Make sure to think through your day and ask about what you'll need, including space for a coat check in colder months and easy access for any physically disabled or elderly guests.

- **Ask for recommendations for vendors,** but do some research on your own as well. Interview caterers and ask for any hidden costs—such as a charge for bringing in cooking equipment. Do site walk-throughs with potential designers and other vendors to determine possible problem areas, such as power requirements and storage, in advance. Walk-through meetings are a great way to see how designers look at space and scale, and whether you hire them or not, you're likely to glean a few good ideas. When the time comes, ask for a written list of questions from each of your vendors so you can follow up with answers from the loft's management.

- **Check out lighting and power** as well as air-conditioning and heating in the space. You'll want to know well before the big day what to expect. Many lofts have beautiful daytime light because of their huge windows, but only functional lighting at night. A friend told me about a loft wedding she attended where she was seated directly in front of a powerful air conditioner. She shivered all night.

- **An up-front financial plan is a must.** Prices range widely for everything from coffee cups to chair cushions, so let your vendors know how much you have to spend right off the bat. If you're not sure, try to have at least a range in mind, as it can be difficult for designers and other vendors to make an appropriate proposal without some idea of your budget goals. Express your design priorities and identify the areas that aren't as important to you. That way, vendors can let you know if your projections are realistic and they'll show you only the options that fit into your price range.

keep it simple and stunning

- **Opt for strong colors** over pastels.
- **Consider simple white tablecloths** with bold runners in a fine fabric.
- **Avoid wispy wildflowers** in favor of vibrant, linear blossoms or masses of classics like roses or tulips.
- **For centerpieces,** float a single giant cattleya orchid or other large flower; or focus on candles rather than flowers.
- **Rectangular dinner tables** are festive and fresh. Make sure they're at least 36" wide to allow room for plates, glasses, and decorations.
- **Follow through with different details.** Use materials that relate to the building or the neighborhood. Or, find an image of the space from its factory days and scan or copy it to use as an accent on your menu cards or programs.

reality check

- Planning and decorating a loft party requires extra logistic expertise. Request help from the venue or your vendors when it comes to planning the number of tables that will fit comfortably, the flow of the party, etc.

- Don't deal with all the rentals yourself. Your caterer or designer should provide that service and you should count on them to make sure you haven't forgotten anything, from forks to coat-check tickets. But do ask your vendor to provide detailed estimates as soon as possible for delivery, rentals, the costs of power and lighting, etc.. If you're not sure about the guest count, estimate a little higher than you think (10% is a safe buffer). There are many costs associated with bringing everything you need into a raw space, and it pays to know sooner rather than later what the total will be.

- Avoid booking a loft space which is still "under renovation." There are many new event lofts popping up in both urban and suburban areas, and often you can request a better deal if you book in advance of an opening. But you don't want to find out a week before your big day that there are no windows or plumbing fixtures yet.

- Unlike hotels or restaurants, lofts usually don't provide a day-of-event coordinator to oversee the arrival of photographers, band, florist, etc. Ask your catering company if they will provide a coordinator or think seriously about hiring a freelance wedding coordinator—many are available for wedding-week or wedding-day-only rates. This may seem like a luxury, but it relieves you of the stress of making sure all your service providers are on time, on track, and in order, so you won't have to worry. And that can be worth a lot!

pink
orchid
tini

pink
bubble
bliss

pink
lemon
rita

We worked with Olivier Cheng Catering and Events to create food and drink accents that would match the modern style of this wedding. Our Pink Drink Bar featured three very different cocktails, to suit any taste (above). Lucite hors d'oeuvre trays were lined with specialty papers or decorated with floating flowers to highlight the bite-sized delights (opposite).

● **Serve foods from beautifully arranged buffet stations,** rather than in a formal, sit-down style. This is often less expensive and it encourages mingling among the guests. But do set your tables with silver, glasses, and napkins rather than offering super-casual and cumbersome silverware and napkin rollups.

- **If you're untraditional,** opt for a beautiful dessert table (or even passed petits fours served on a tray) rather than a wedding cake.

- **If permitted, use pipes or fixtures** to hang simple lanterns over the dance floor. Do check in advance for any regulations or restrictions.

where to splurge

- **Lofts are sometimes in deserted** or borderline-unsafe neighborhoods. Arrange a secure parking lot or, better yet, valet parking, to ensure the comfort level of guests who may not be familiar with the area.

- **Ask your caterer to bring hundreds** of simple, clear votives and use them to line the windowsills in the loft, if permitted. Have candles everywhere, except unattended areas. (Most venues that host events are required to have fire safety equipment on hand, but it's a good idea to ask in advance.)

- **Spend money on your linens,** tabletop details, and chairs. Choose elegant plates and fine linens with coordinating chair covers. Place a single blossom on every napkin, or better yet, print a poem on Japanese rice paper to adorn each place setting.

- **If your loft lobby is less-than-gorgeous,** post a violinist (or an electric guitarist) near the elevator, along with a few candles on stands to welcome your guests.

Logistics: **DIFFICULT** | Décor: **MODERATE** | Personalizing: **SIMPLE**

beach

A soft breeze from the south. Rippling grasses along the dunes. Spirited whispers of waves, the warmth of white sand and golden sun. The vastness of the ocean landscape becomes a symbol of your never-ending love as you welcome your guests with gracious natural details and casual charm.

sun, sand, simple?

Couples who are married at the beach dream of a setting that is more than just a location. You may feel that the sea is a powerful presence, even a witness, along with your family and friends, to the commitment you are about to make to each other.

Is the beach for you? Most brides and grooms who choose a beach wedding are outdoorsy people with a love of nature and a flair for unaffected style. Perhaps you grew up at the shore. Or you met each other on a beach weekend. Whatever your reasons for marrying at the ocean's edge, chances are you want your celebration to be at least somewhat casual, with an emphasis on the beauty and magnificent simplicity of your surroundings.

There are several types of beach weddings. One of the easiest and most exotic is the weekend getaway wedding, organized through a good hotel in a gorgeous spot. This type of

With a stunning backdrop like this, you don't need much more than a few rented benches and some wind-proof lanterns. Two sand-filled galvanized pails holding long, undulating grasses helped frame the space, and dried starfish kept the blue cotton hankies from fluttering away. You might want to welcome guests with a weekend itinerary package (ours is from twentyandseven), complete with sunglasses to wear to the party (see page 148).

affair is best for a limited number of guests, as it generally involves a bit of travel and extra expense for those who attend. It can be economical for the bride and groom, however, as fewer guests means less money spent on food, drink, and décor.

Many fine hotels offer a complete package of services—from accommodations to officiants, from flowers to cocktails and food—to make the process easier. Of course, you must do your homework to find referrals through friends, chambers of commerce, or travel or wedding magazines. And distance might force you to give up controlling every single decorative detail. The good news is that if you opt for this type of wedding, you have the benefit of one-stop planning, with the added possibility of a weekend—or a week—full of activities.

If you're lucky enough to have the beach in your backyard, you might consider a casual classic clambake or barbecue celebration—a ceremony using a colorful cabana as a backdrop, followed by an informal party with a microbrew bar set up on a surfboard, and a sandcastle contest for the kids.

If you are truly going casual, it is possible to have family and friends do the cooking—steaming lobsters, or assembling a potluck buffet served on picnic tables borrowed from the neighbors or rented from a local shop. This wedding is simplest for a small or medium-sized group, as a sudden storm or windy conditions might require

WAVES OF

COLORS: Think sun and sand. Instead of nautical blue, opt for spicy citrus tones or shades of green and naturals against white.

FLOWERS: Hydrangea, grasses, daisies, garden roses, solidago and sunflowers or exotics like protea, echiveria, and leukodendron.

MATERIALS: Galvanized pails, bright plastics, wood, natural fibers, sand, stones, and shells.

HOW IT FEELS: Fun, festive, casual, powerful, elemental, organic, unfussy.

CROSS-REFERENCE: The Tent, Vineyard, and Farm chapters are all good sources of logistical information for beach brides and grooms.

you to bring everything—and everyone—inside quickly. It's similar to an at-home celebration, as you'll need to make sure you're close enough to a house or covered area to transport the whole party easily and quickly, and at a moments' notice. (See the Tent chapter for more information.)

A catered beach wedding is the best choice for larger groups, or for brides and grooms who don't want family and friends to have to lift a finger. Using a caterer ensures a more sophisticated and stress-free event, even if you are serving very

Use ocean-inspired accents, such as sea glass, in your décor. Try not to use objects or materials that could damage your surroundings (above). During cocktail hour, we moved the ceremony benches to the dinner area. Benches or garden-style chairs are your best bet for stable seating on the beach. And low, sturdy glassware, along with wind-resistant décor, is a good idea (opposite).

casual foods, and offers the opportunity to create a more elegant menu if you desire.

At a beach celebration, every single item must be trucked in or carried on foot. If you use chairs on the beach, avoid the sand-sinking bamboo styles: instead opt for more stable folding wooden "garden" chairs or benches which most party rental companies offer.

If you are hosting your wedding at an unfamiliar beach location, an experienced caterer is a must, as logistics will become an issue for your reception. Depending on your location, a tent may be required, which complicates matters even more (see the Tent chapter for more information), but is strongly recommended if shelter is not readily available. Make sure to talk to your caterer about regulations and permits—every town and village has specific requirements about driving, cooking, music, entertaining, and erecting tents on beachfront property.

know your setting

● **Many beaches are public spaces** with long lists of regulations. Some don't permit any alcohol, some require applications to be processed and fees to be paid, and some are privately held and off-limits. Glass may be prohibited, and garbage disposal may be an issue. Check with local authorities regarding permits, rules, and facilities.

We created this signature crushed ice cocktail with vodka and Blue Curacao, and served it in wax paper cones tucked into a bin of crushed ice (above). A casual seafood buffet (opposite, above). The Clam Man Caterers of Southampton, New York, created this bountiful display of salads, vegetables, and shellfish. An old rowboat filled with ice and propped up on sturdy sawhorses makes a great bar (opposite, below).

- **Beach logistics are often challenging.** Make plans for delivery and shelter, adequate parking, and bathroom facilities. If your party will last until after dark, you may need to provide lighting with torches, outdoor lanterns, or even generators, if permitted.

- **More than with any other outdoor event,** you and your guests are exposed to the elements. Have sunscreen, sunglasses, and insect repellent on hand, and make sure your party space is covered to protect your guests from sunburn and high winds.

- **As with a tent wedding,** you will most likely need to bring in all your tables, chairs, and dinnerware. Find out what your location and caterer provides to avoid hidden costs and hassles. Choose basic (even paper or plastic) utensils. You'll have fewer headaches if you keep it truly casual.

- **Beaches can be difficult** for the very young, the elderly, and those with physical disabilities that might make it hard to navigate the sand. Keep your guests in mind when planning entrances, walkways, the location of bathrooms, etc.

- **It might be tough** to maintain a strict party perimeter. Be prepared for dogs off leashes, small children and other beachcombers to walk or run through (or near) your celebration. If you're on a public beach, you might also encounter noise from radios or other recreational sounds from fellow beach lovers.

- **Know your high and low tides** and plan your celebration accordingly, to avoid a washout.

keep it simple and stunning

- **Choose solids or basic patterns** for your linens. Muted, earthy tones, as well as thick stripes, polka dots, and alternating colors work wonderfully.

- **Keep flower arrangements natural and low.** Floating blossoms in simple wooden bowls or armfuls of hydrangea or daisies are easy and appropriate. You can even get away with a wide hurricane glass holding a single fat pillar candle, with a few blooms tossed in whimsically.

- **Serve buffet-style foods** at room temperature or on ice. Poached salmon, pasta salad, finger sandwiches, and marinated grilled vegetables are all great ideas. Add seaweed, shells, and other seaside elements for a splashy accent. Use giant clamshells as serving dishes and make as much of your finger-friendly food as possible.

- **Shop at garden centers** or discount stores for outdoor candles and lanterns or tiki torches. Use citronella oil or candles wherever possible to help with insect control.

- **Avoid blow-overs** by filling vases and candle holders with sand for extra weight.

- **Include "beach chic" dress instructions** on your invitations to let guests know it's okay to be festive but comfortable.

- **Locate your ceremony space** in front of a row of dunes, or tuck bamboo poles into the sand

- Your bridal gown should be shorter than full length and casual. Bare feet or shoes you can kick off are appropriate. And don't make your groom—or your guests—wear black tie attire.

- Avoid fancy fly-away escort cards and super-formal seating assignments. Encourage open seating (with convenient spots for anyone who has mobility problems) or use a chalkboard and easel for your table chart.

- Offering food and drink in a setting with no running water or electricity presents its challenges. Unless your wedding is very small, the beach is in your backyard, *and* you're feeling really ambitious, hire a good caterer with beach experience.

- If possible, host one production meeting with all your service providers (florist, caterer, etc.) present at the wedding location. This way, you can address any logistical or aesthetic issues in advance. Walk through your party space and discuss where bars and buffets will be set up, where tenting will be situated if necessary, and how food and drinks will be prepared, transported, and served.

old blues and other contemporary colors can work when all is flowing and moving, but it's best to take your cues from nature. This simple centerpiece, which incorporates floating flowers and pillar candles with sea glass, would also work well in any modern setting, such as a loft or tent.

and hang a billowy curtain as a backdrop. Avoid top-heavy or tall arrangements which might be blown over by a strong wind.

- **The beach makes people** want to move around and mingle: hire a steel drum band or other upbeat musical group to add party magic.

- **Create a Sand Bar** with two sawhorses and a surfboard. Serve a few light drinks—a sunny juice-based cocktail and a few microbrews, plus water and sodas for the kids.

- **Give your flower girls beach pails** filled with colorful rose petals. And don't forget kid-sized shovels so they can easily sprinkle and scatter blossoms as they move down the aisle.

where to splurge

- **Serve the best of the ocean's treasures**— steamed chilled lobster, crab legs, giant prawns, even a caviar bar!

- **Rent small wireless microphones** for the ceremony. Crashing waves, squawking gulls, even the wind can make it impossible for your guests to hear those romantic vows you're exchanging. And they want to hear every word!

- **Arrive in high style:** charter speedboats or a yacht to bring you and the bridal party to the ceremony. This can be great fun for you and your attendants, especially if you can spend an hour or so touring the local waters.

a basketful of beach blankets and a pile of pillows invite guests to relax near a sunset bonfire (above). As the sun disappears, square dinner tables set with blue burlap tablecloths and coordinating rented china await (opposite). Be sure to add tiki torches, lanterns, or outdoor lighting if your celebration will continue after dark.

Logistics: **DIFFICULT** | Décor: **SIMPLE** | Personalizing: **SIMPLE**

farm

Gracious nature surrounds your ceremony. A single fiddler serenades your wedding party as you walk down a leaf-covered aisle towards a majestic old tree adorned with pretty ribbons. You welcome your guests with warm spiced wine by the fireplace and a delightful menu of seasonal, local foods. Whether you prefer square dancing or the classic sounds of Patsy Cline and company, a sense of history and a connection to the land infuse your celebration with an easy, natural spirit and much romance.

a dahlia and rose bouquet mirrors the colors of the autumn leaves (above). This ceremony, set at Gedney Farm in New Marlborough, Massachusetts, celebrates the beauty and majesty of a tree bedecked with ribbons (opposite). Chairs from the farm's restaurant and mason jar lanterns (made by twisting wire around the jar's lip) line a leaf-covered aisle.

all-natural

A farm wedding can be elegant or casual, family-style or festive, classic or contemporary, depending upon your location and your preferences. From working dude ranches to equestrian centers to organic vegetable fields and renovated Normandy barns, more and more farm properties are opening their land, as well as their barns and other buildings for use as reception venues.

I was a guest at a farm wedding recently and was absolutely charmed by the simplicity, beauty, and natural spontaneity of the celebration. The ceremony was to be held outside, with the couple exchanging vows near a pretty stream. When a storm suddenly struck, the original plan had to be scrapped and a new one improvised inside the barn. Everyone pitched in and brought pails of wildflowers in to line the aisle, and the sound of rain on the roof added magic and romance to the ceremony. The bride and groom took the last-minute changes in stride and had a wonderful party as a result.

There is a certain easiness of spirit about a farm, a sense of genuine welcome and warmth that makes it the perfect setting for a wedding. The idea that things are growing and taking root all around creates a magical, bountiful atmosphere. I've always thought it good luck for a bride and groom to be surrounded by such a rich abundance of life and nature when beginning their new life together.

Farms come in all shapes and sizes, from working mills and dairy barns to renovated former

farms that have been equipped and appointed for the most elegant celebrations. If you're considering a farm wedding, you're likely an outdoorsy couple with a strong feeling for fresh foods, fresh air, and natural, traditional surroundings. You might like horses or be environmentally conscious, or maybe you just love the scale and style of a loft-like barn, with its post-and-beam structure and soaring ceilings.

Often farms that host weddings also have an inn or rooms associated with their property.

Many couples choose to host a wedding weekend, with the rehearsal dinner and post-wedding brunch all held on the property. The advantage of this type of situation is that, generally, the banquet staff or management of these venues will coordinate all of your wedding events, saving you the time and trouble of dealing with multiple facilities and vendors. Purchasing a package of events, whatever your location, is always a good idea from a financial standpoint and can result in significant savings.

There are a number of important issues to consider when looking at possible farm locations for your wedding. Will this be a "weekend getaway" wedding, with the guests traveling to a secluded area, or is there a farm facility near your home or closer to a metropolitan area? This will affect your travel plans and can also have an impact on available activities for your guests during the wedding weekend.

Are there enough guest rooms to accommodate all of your party, or are there additional lodgings available nearby? It is wise to consider how your guests will travel back to their rooms at the party's

DOWN TO EARTH
inspiration

COLORS: Choose natural shades like oatmeal, chocolate, sage, and wheat as your foundation, then accent with herbal greens or flowers in shades of orange, red, or yellow.

FLOWERS: Plants, seeds, corn, wheat, wildflowers, branches, grasses, apples, pears, potatoes, pumpkins— focus on the bounty of the earth for your decorative elements.

MATERIALS: Wood, glass jars, ceramics, clay, grass, baskets.

HOW IT FEELS: Gracious, earthy, relaxed, rooted, seasonal.

CROSS-REFERENCE: See the Country Inn, Botanic Garden, and Tent chapters for more information and inspiration.

tables are set in one of Gedney Farm's renovated Normandy barns. Chocolate velvet and faux suede tablecloths alternate throughout the space. The centerpieces, clustered bowls filled with pears and apples, can be donated after the party.

heavy bubbled stemware and china with a gold leaf motif set the tables (above). With store-bought card stock, a rubber stamp, and pretty liner paper, we created these homemade invitations, place cards, and gift tags (opposite, above). The National Arbor Day Foundation sells inexpensive "gift trees," seedlings packed in plastic tubes, which make great guest favors (opposite, below).

end, especially if you'll be serving alcohol. Are there taxis or shuttle buses available, or will guests be responsible for driving? What are the roads like?

Of course you'll want to know if there are multiple events or weddings scheduled for your date or weekend. Some couples prefer that theirs be the only celebration taking place. If there are other events, be sure to coordinate timing and logistics—I recommend starting at least an hour before or after another event to avoid parking problems and delays. And you should inquire about catering arrangements; some farms have facilities and staff to prepare your special menu, while others require you to arrange for everything yourself.

This brings up another key aspect to consider. What kind of farm wedding would you prefer? Do you envision hay-bale benches and an easy, casual buffet of grilled and barbecued food, with lots of dancing, and lots of family and kids? Or do you want a stately farm feast, with velvet tablecloths, sparkling cider, an orchestra, and a menu of organic favorites such as sweet peas, heirloom tomatoes, and free-range chicken?

Imagine yourself on your wedding day and try to picture the overall feeling you'd like to create. If you find yourself drawn to the idea of a barn dance shindig, follow that all the way through with friendly, easy choices of everything from your invitations to your wedding dress, from the table settings to the cocktail hour, which might involve hayrides for your guests and country music CDs as party favors.

If you envision a more stately evening, opt for elegant colors, soft lighting, a tailored menu of local produce, simple fine china and linens, and perhaps seedling trees as gifts for your guests. Whichever style of celebration you prefer, always make choices based on colors in nature and, preferably, in season. Staying in step with your surroundings will provide much visual power and an overall sense of harmony.

One last note: a farm wedding is a perfect place to use and celebrate foods, decorations, and other items which are handmade. If you are comfortable with a computer and a rubber stamp, you can make pretty invitations, programs, or place cards without a lot of trouble. If the farm produces cheese, preserves, or pancake mix, offer them as favors for your guests. Order bushels of apples, pears, or tomatoes from the farm to decorate your tables and give them to guests as a tasty souvenir. Stay away from anything too fancy or frivolous and focus on the natural beauty that surrounds you.

know your setting

 **Many farms feature older buildings** that are full of charm, but also vulnerable to changes in the weather. It can be almost impossible to air-condition a barn or stable, so be sure you're comfortable with whatever Mother Nature may bring. And do your research as to average temperatures, rainfall, etc. for your wedding date.

- **As with a loft or tent wedding,** you may need to bring in all your tables, chairs, silverware—even power and light in many cases. Investigate first to avoid hidden costs and hassles, and choose simple, unfussy tableware.

- **As with any outdoor wedding,** have a back-up plan for your ceremony if you'll be exchanging vows outside. Since farms often have buildings placed at some distance from each other, think about how your guests will move from one place to another in the event of rain.

- **Farms are working businesses.** Ask about what activities will be in progress on your wedding day. Will heavy equipment be in use or in sight? If the farm raises or stables livestock, will there be unpleasant odors or disruptive sounds? You'll want to know this ahead of time.

keep it simple and stunning

- **Host a truly informal wedding.** Serve hamburgers or barbecued ribs with great beers, and arrange your seating at picnic-style tables.

- **Keep your dress code in line** with your party. Let guests know they should wear comfortable shoes and specify cowboy casual or "elegant organic" as a clue to proper attire on your invitations.

This barn features a beautiful fireplace with hanging decorative objects. We added bittersweet vines and pillar candles to warm up a lounge area for serving spiced mulled wine (page 160). If you prefer a floral centerpiece, stick to seasonal, unfussy blooms, such as dahlias, roses, and cockscomb, arranged in simple, earthy containers (opposite).

- Don't pick a farm that's too far away from a town or village with at least one hotel. Since a farm wedding is often a weekend getaway, you'll want to make sure your guests have a place to stay during the festivities.

- Avoid planning a farm wedding during extreme weather months, unless you've visited the site and know it has been weather-proofed.

- It's not advisable to book a farm location that hasn't been used for a number of weddings before. While you may be able to negotiate a good price, you'll want to be certain they can handle the basic logistics such as parking, plumbing, local zoning regulations, etc.

- Many farmers rent out space, but do not supervise or run events themselves. Find out if someone will be on-site to deal with any problems that might arise.

Chef Peter Platt created a seasonal butternut squash soup for this wedding, and added a special romantic touch—delicate floating hearts of crème fraiche (above). This tea-stained cake with fondant and stenciled accents was designed by Elisa Strauss of Confetti Cakes to echo antique textiles (opposite).

- **Gather wildflowers or seasonal plants** from a nearby farmers' market in simple bushel baskets, or make centerpieces out of produce from the farm.

- **Ask about using props** the farm already has. Decorate a wheelbarrow to display favors of canned vegetables or seed packets. Or use a stack of hay bales or two old wooden ladders adorned with flowers to flank your ceremony space.

- **Plan activities during cocktail hour.** How about a horseshoe throwing contest or a pony ride for the kids?

- **Hire a live, country-style or bluegrass band.** Ask for washboards, fiddles, and guitars, rather than big band sounds or modern synthesizers.
- **If the weather is nice,** encourage guests to stroll from the ceremony to the reception. Line the walkway with citronella lanterns made from canning jars, and keep insect repellent on hand.
- **If you will have assigned seating,** string a clothesline between two trees or along a fence, and attach your escort cards with clothespins.
- **If possible, incorporate the farm's products** into your menu—honey, goat cheese, corn, baby organic lettuces, heirloom tomatoes—using the best of the season to personalize your wedding feast.

where to splurge

- **Book the best square-dance caller** in the county. You and your guests will be dancing all night!
- **Hire enough wagons and drivers** to take all your guests on a sunset hayride before dinner, and have waiters standing by with trays of spicy apple cider when they return for dinner.
- **Deliver welcome baskets** of tasty "homegrown" snacks to your guests' hotel rooms. Include products from your farm plus other local specialties and information about the area, its history, and activities your friends and family might enjoy.

Logistics: **DIFFICULT** | Décor: **DIFFICULT** | Personalizing: **SIMPLE**

tent

Your guests are ushered through billowy curtains to a spicy cocktail "lounge" adorned with Chinese lanterns, inviting sofas, couches, and a drop-dead view of the ocean. When it's time for dinner, a path leads them toward the most elegant dining room ever, magically situated in the woods under a giant moon, protected from the elements by a canvas ceiling washed with soft light. This is your wedding vision, brought to life in your perfect setting. A gentle breeze wafts up as you take to the dance floor, and you can't help thinking all the planning was *so* worth it.

your blank
canvas

Most wedding venues provide at least the basics—shelter, facilities, an architectural or decorative approach to start you on your way. A wedding in a tent, on the other hand, is the ultimate "bring-your-own" situation, where anything is possible and nothing is provided.

Some of the most beautiful weddings I've designed have been held in tents. These weddings have also been the most logistically challenging and the most costly. Like lofts, tents offer the opportunity to work freely with color. Spicy, bold colors or Zen serenity, funky bohemian décor or modern minimalism—it's really up to you. Since you can specify sizes, shapes, and layouts (bordered only by the limits of your property and your budget), it's possible to create lounge tents, dining tents, cocktail tents, ceremony tents—whatever suits your wishes and needs.

There is usually a very good reason why a couple wants or needs to construct a tent on a given site—nearby water, a beautiful piece of property, a

beautifully lit, peaked-roof tent, such as this one designed for a wedding at the bride's family's country home, provides a stunning "wow" moment when guests enter the space. Softly glowing lanterns, curtains, floral accents at entrances, and special details such as ivory chair covers infused this wedding with a one-of-a kind feeling.

family home. Generally, brides and grooms who consider a tent wedding either want to be married outside or to hold their receptions in a very specific, very special place that is not necessarily designed to host a large number of guests.

Through my experiences in planning and designing many tent weddings, however, I've noticed that very few couples (or their families) understand what a complicated undertaking a tent wedding is. I'm not talking about a wedding at a facility such as a country inn, an historic mansion, or a botanic garden when there is a permanent tent on site. Weddings in these venues can be quite easy to plan and execute, as the property is already designed to accommodate guests, and the staff is comfortable with all of the inherent logistic issues and considerations in moving the activity to the tent area.

But the wedding which is held on a property or in a locale where a tent is not already provided (usually a large "at-home" celebration with too many guests to squeeze inside the house) is more complex. For you must provide your guests with everything they need to celebrate comfortably, just as if they were invited into your home, or a hotel or private club.

A lovely couple I once worked with initially said to me, "All we want is a simple backyard wedding." I agreed that this was a wonderful idea, and visions of a casual afternoon barbecue began to dance in my head—until they mentioned that their guest list was already over 175! At that point, in my mind the word "simple" was replaced with the word "tent."

Constructing a tent is actually designing and erecting a temporary building. The most important element a tent provides is shelter, so it must function in exactly the way any other shelter would. There must be cooking facilities, bathrooms, electricity, lights, emergency exits—not to mention forks, knives, glasses, tablecloths, chairs, and, if you so desire, a dance floor. If there is a house very nearby it is possible to use these bathroom and kitchen facilities, but residential kitchens and limited septic capacities can create major problems for even a modest-sized wedding celebration.

Usually, the couple wants to incorporate the outdoors if the tent is located in a pretty setting, so that the ceremony, and possibly the cocktail hour also, are held outside, weather permitting. This requires extra planning to ensure a smooth celebration in the case of rain or cold.

The key is to work with a reputable tent company. My colleagues at Northeast Tent Productions in Connecticut suggest having a representative come out to survey the property and prepare a detailed proposal outlining all the equipment and accoutrements you might need and want. This visit is usually complimentary. Ask your planner, caterer, designer, or a friend for a few recommendations, and make sure you're comparing the same equipment and services when you're evaluating budgets. Look at costs for generators, walkways, flooring, and on-site staffing for the wedding day. Remember that, as with most services, the cheapest bid is not necessarily the best one to accept. You want to be sure that there will not be a lot of "additional" costs added on the day of the ceremony.

There are all kinds of issues to think about when choosing a tent. What kind of tent will it be? A basic canopy or an elegant, peaked roof "empire" tent? Will you have clear or decorative side walls? Will there be a floor? I strongly recommend some kind of flooring in all cases except where wet weather is a very remote possibility. If the ground is damp, guests might ruin their shoes—or twist their ankles. There are several types of flooring options, from "portable" segments which are laid directly over the ground, to sturdy sub-plywood constructions which are more expensive and luxurious. Floor coverings are available in everything from Astroturf to wall-to-wall carpeting. Find out what's available from your tent company.

I've had clients express concern about ruining their lawns by putting up a floor for their tents, but Steve Bombino of Northeast Tent Productions tells me that generally, a quality floor actually protects the grass underneath. That being said, you must be prepared for some lawn damage anytime you are erecting a large structure on the grass and inviting upwards of 100 guests to walk and dance on the property.

The bottom line is that a tent wedding is a major production. Usually, the tent will be constructed the week before your wedding, with last-minute adjustments to accommodate the weather and your wishes made on or just before the big day. If it is raining or the ground is damp, you might want to have umbrellas on hand, or add walkways and canopies on any unpaved areas near the tent entrances.

If your tent is connected to or near your home, you might want to host an open-house-style cocktail hour, or have champagne and hors d'oeuvres on the lawn or around a pool. Just make sure to have a rain plan and a clear, well-lit path between your spaces.

Think through the details of your tent wedding as much as possible. You don't want to complicate your celebration, but you do want to make your honored family and friends as comfortable as possible. Just make sure to talk through both Plan A and Plan B well in advance, so that your tent and catering staff and wedding party know the alternatives and are able to quickly adjust to a change in plans.

The hanging amaranthus and green cymbidium orchids, which accent this cattail and birch *huppah*, billow in the soft breeze on a late-summer afternoon (opposite, above). Small swags of foxtail grasses with a single green dendrobium orchid adorn white folding chairs flanking the aisle (opposite, below).

Most reputable tent companies provide on-site supervision on the wedding day so that adjustments can be made to remove or replace the sides panels of the tent to accommodate changing weather. I highly recommend that you insist upon this, as weather changes are common from day to evening, and temperatures fluctuate when large groups of people assemble in a space. If chilly weather is predicted, your tent company can provide portable heaters, and for warmer evenings, I

inspiration

COLORS: A tent is like a loft, which means it's a great setting for either bold colors or sleek, bridal whites and other neutral tones.

FLOWERS: Pick a theme. Wildflowers? Modern blooms? Geometric arrangements, or classical posies? Look at the flowers or botanical elements which will surround your tent for inspiration, or just use your imagination.

MATERIALS: Consistency is the key here. If you choose glass accents, don't use woodsy baskets. If you prefer moss and terra-cotta, stick with earthier materials. Limiting choices gives you power.

HOW IT FEELS: Personal, custom-made, al fresco, special, one-of-a-kind.

CROSS-REFERENCE: See the Beach, Loft, and Hotel chapters for logistics, as well as just about any chapter for decorative ideas, from traditional to modern.

Continuing with the ceremony's cattail theme, drawn from the landscape, we created giant modern arrangements of hundreds of these tall, reed-like stems, to flank the beginning of the aisle. The ceremony was held outside, but a rain contingency plan to move décor into the cocktail tent in the case of inclement weather was in place.

do suggest fans be placed in the corners of your tent, just to keep air circulating. Air conditioning a tent is very expensive—I recommend it only in exceptional situations.

You can decorate your tent however you like, but I usually suggest not to try to turn it into something other than a tent. Avoid heavily draped and garland-covered "over-the-top" designs in favor of pretty linens, simple but beautiful flowers, and candles (if permitted). And don't forget lighting design if the wedding will take place after sunset.

know your setting

- **Tents require more decision-making** than any other wedding location. If you know what you want or at least what you like, you'll be fine. If you're not great at making choices about forks, portable toilets, and outdoor lighting, or just not interested in that level of detail, you'll want to either leave it to the professionals or consider hosting your wedding in a simpler setting.

- **Get a tent company representative** involved as early as possible. These experts can evaluate your property and make recommendations, plus provide budget details and vendor recommendations which may help you in your decision-making process. Many can arrange for generators, lighting, even bathroom facilities, which makes for easier planning.

- **Every city, town, or village** has a list of regulations for hosting a tent event. Your tent company will likely help you with some of these, but you'll want to know yourself what forms need to be filed, which inspections (fire, building, etc.) will take place once the tents are erected, and what is not permitted (gas cooking equipment, candles, non-fire-retardant fabrics, etc.). There are also rules about live music, residential parking, even party ending times—find out in advance.

- **Know that there will likely be some damage** to your lawn. When trucks, work crews, and lots of guests are using your property over the course of a week or so, it is inevitable that you'll experience some wear and tear above and beyond what is normal. You would be wise to consider reseeding the lawn afterwards as one of your budget items.

- **Before your wedding,** you may choose to spray for mosquitoes and other pests, but some pesticides may pose health risks and can interfere with setup times. Citronella candles and torches may help if permitted. If your property is anywhere near wildlife or water, consider having it examined for animals and pests. Call your local animal control agency for more information. This may sound funny, but I've had a family of raccoons destroy table decorations, and my staff once encountered nests of snakes—yes, snakes—while setting up for a tent wedding.

- **Be sure to make adequate arrangements** for garbage disposal and after-wedding cleanup. One of the biggest problems I've encountered

is a lack of appropriate garbage disposal. Make sure you have dumpsters, or that each vendor is responsible for removing their own garbage, as well as for returning to the site after the wedding to ensure proper cleanup.

- **Have a rain plan.** This may seem obvious, but make sure that your tent will allow for a covered ceremony in case of inclement weather. Discuss the flow of transitions (from guest arrival through ceremony, cocktails, and dinner) with all pertinent service providers to minimize any impact on your guests' comfort.

- **Know that tent budgets** are inclined to increase. If you decide at the last minute to add more tents, a floor, heaters, or fans, there will be a cost. Try to examine all the options up-front so you'll be clear about what to expect in case you do decide to add or change details.

keep it simple and stunning

- **Don't try to turn your tent** into a hotel ballroom or a reproduction of Versailles. Let your natural surroundings inspire you and focus on color, pretty linens, and unique table decorations, as well as a good caterer.

- **Decorate the entrance to your tent.** One of the most lovely, luxuriously simple escort card designs

he bride's family's personal chef oversaw all the food preparations for this buffet-style wedding, and we created modern, food-inspired décor with branches, grasses, and green fruits and vegetables to accent the presentations (above). Modern white pedestals hold glass cylinders filled with submerged oranges and giant green hanging amaranthus, flanking a curtain-draped entrance to the cocktail tent (opposite).

With a cotton tablecloth and just three types of flowers, we created a simpler version of the luxurious bride's table on the next page (above). For this wedding, we used custom duppioni silk tablecloths in earthy green, linen napkins in ivory, and added a single green chrysanthemum at each place setting. A row of simple bouquets in burgundy and green was arranged along the center of the table. Frosted glass chargers and modern flatware completed the look (opposite).

I've created was for a couple who were both musicians. We covered the tented entrance canopy to the main tent with curly willow branches and hung 200 individual wind chimes from the branches, each personalized with a guest's name and table number. The chimes swung softly from colorful ribbons in the September breeze, and staff members cut them down as guests made their way to dinner. This musical card/favor was a charming and personal touch.

- **Insist on a floor.** Remember that if it rains, even a few days before the wedding, a soggy lawn under your tent can ruin tablecloths, guests' shoes, and everyone's comfort level. You might want to add walkways and canopies at key points to make it more comfortable for you and your guests.

- **Serve a menu in the style that works** best for your caterer. If buffets are her forte, create beautiful food station presentations incorporating fruits and vegetables. For a more formal feel, you can serve a sit-down dinner, but limit your choices and courses. Remember that the logistics in a tent make it a bit harder to serve guests quickly and easily, so keep that in mind, and ask your caterer for menu recommendations.

- **Treat each tent separately,** and create a mood which fits the purpose. The wedding we featured in this chapter, in a tent by P.J. McBride, was designed as an outdoor ceremony that could be moved into the cocktail tent if necessary (fortunately the weather was perfect!). For cocktail hour, we used spicy pinks and oranges and

- I can't stress how important it is to have a planning staff for a tent wedding. There are just so many details—construction issues, permits, weather considerations, alternate plans, parking arrangements, etc. Ask your designer or caterer if they can provide or recommend an experienced professional. Then check references and find someone you really like. After all, you'll be spending a lot of time with that person, including one of the most important days of your life.

- Insist on at least one "production" meeting for your vendors. Your planner should organize and host this meeting, with a timeline for vendor arrival and a list of questions or issues to address with each service provider. This way, everyone has contact information and an opportunity to confirm details in advance, as well as to know who is in charge of what. This also promotes teamwork, and it makes the set-up process less confusing and friendlier, if crews and supervisors know one another.

- Purchase extra insurance. Building a tent and hosting a large group of people on your property necessarily imposes certain risks. Most homeowner's policies can be supplemented for a one-time event. Also, insist on copies of insurance certificates for all of your service providers, and ask that you be named as "additional insured."

- Above all else, get the details in writing. Equipment, arrival and setup times, number of staff, garbage removal and cleanup plans, along with alternate plans for inclement weather. Although I recommend this for every wedding, it is never more important than in a tent celebration, where you are, in effect, building your wedding location.

arranged seating areas, with a hanging escort card tree—a colorful space that also served as a lounge for later on. The dinner tent was the height of modern elegance, decorated in ivory and shades of green, with simple Chinese lanterns and geometric vases filled with flowers in green and a deep chocolate-red.

where to splurge

- **Create lounges.** A cocktail or ceremony tent can be transformed into a great party space with a few minor adjustments. Pick a theme—for one tent wedding, I designed two different lounge tents: the first, designed for the couple and their friends, was filled with pillows, candles, and incense, and I called it "The Moroccan Lounge." For the parents, I revamped the cocktail tent into a sleek, clubby space dubbed "The Zen Cigar Lounge." These were great gathering spots throughout the evening and made for perfect, intimate places to continue the party when the majority of guests had departed.

- **Hire a good lighting designer.** Most tent companies provide basic lighting for safety and some have equipment or arrangements with vendors to provide more complex lighting. Because a tent is a blank, open space, lighting can be truly transformational. You can project a beautiful light stencil on the tent ceiling, and add accent

lighting on ponds, trees, stairs, and nearby architectural elements. Lanterns strung from the ceiling are dramatic, adding color and scale to your design, while spot-lighting tables and buffets will enhance the look of your centerpieces and displays. (For more information about lighting design, see the Hotel chapter.)

This living-room-like cocktail lounge, filled with couches, ottomans, and a very popular basket of ladies' slippers (for tired feet), also functioned as an after-party space as the evening wound down (above, left). An escort card "tree" offers cards dangling from ribbons. Guests' names were arranged alphabetically around the tree (above, right).

acknowledgments

Many people helped me make this book possible. Heartfelt thanks to my agent, Joy Tutela, and to the David Black Literary Agency, for their personal attention and guidance. Eternal gratitude to Leslie Stoker at Stewart, Tabori & Chang, and especially to my editor, Anne Kostick, for sharing her expertise and enthusiasm with a first-time author. Thanks to Ellen Silverman for not only bringing the ideas and moods in this book to life with her brilliant photography, but also being a great friend and collaborator. To Susi Oberhelman, whose design has added so much color and magic to these pages.

My linen maestra, Linda Lieberman of Just Linens Ltd., and the inimitable Lance York of TriServe Party Rentals, loaned me their knowledge and style, as well as every single rented plate, glass, fork, tablecloth, and chair cover on these pages. Thanks to my colleagues at New York City's wholesale flower market: John Kiamos at Associated Cut Flowers; Richard Moore and Lauren Page at G. Page Wholesale Flowers; Eddie and Gus at U.S. Evergreen; and many others, for for working so hard so early in the morning! And thanks to Jackie Fazio and Sally Krause at the Brooklyn Botanic Garden for their assistance.

Antonia Van der Meer and Linda Hirst at *Modern Bride* had faith in my abilities and gave me great design freedom throughout the years. Thanks also to Stephen Scoble, Darcy Miller, and Rebecca Thuss. For organizational inspiration, thanks to Irene Hamburger.

The brides and grooms whose weddings are featured in this book were generous and accommodating, even on the most important day of their lives. Thanks to Ali Marsh, Katie Fogg, and to Lisbeth Scott and Nathan Barr. Special thanks to John and Penny Barr and to Arthur and Linda Carter for their kindness. A deeply felt and special thank you to Diane Fogg, for her endless support and generosity.

It was Alan Tardi who first encouraged me to design flowers, and it was Rocco DiSpirito who gave me the opportunity to design flowers and more for his restaurants, and to be a part of his incredible creative team. To both of these talented chefs, I am truly indebted. I'm grateful also to Carla Lalli Music, Jonathan Hayes, Henry Leutweyler, and Ruba Abu-Nimah. Thanks to John Wilk for his counsel and his poetry; to Brad Paris for the use of his photos; to Abby Weintraub, Eric "DJ Sir Shorty" Meyerson, and John Ballesteros of Vali Music for their help with this project.

Huge thanks to my studio staff, present and former, including Beth Burgess, Lauren Wells, Kim Hirst, Regina Khudyakova, Neftali Molina, Mats Nordman, and to our colleagues Marcella Davoren, Guadalupe Olano, Yoko Mori, Aureliano Morales, and Edmundo Lopez.

Thanks to my mom, Linda Mikhael, and to David Bussen, Mark Dorfman, Dasha Wright, Nissim Israel, Alexander Weck, Ron Schwalb, Samir Chokshi, Eleanor SantoDomingo, and Yoichiro Suzuki. Special thanks to my good friend, Richard Carpiano. And of course, a kiss to everyone at Florent for always making room for me—and my fabric swatches—at the counter.

credits/sources

Each wedding requires many experts, and I am fortunate to work with the best in the business. To each of the location managers, caterers, lighting designers, freelance florists, delivery drivers, bakers, floral supply merchants, and other production assistants who helped make these weddings, and therefore this book, my deepest thanks. I've included contact information for each contributor below, so that couples can take advantage of these great resources.

RESTAURANT

LOCATION:
Django
480 Lexington Avenue
New York, NY 10167
212-871-6600
Special thanks to Missy Rosenthal and
Spencer Rothschild

CAKE:
Cheryl Kleinman Cakes
448 Atlantic Avenue
Brooklyn, NY 11217
718-237-2271

PRIVATE CLUB

LOCATION:
Westchester Country Club
Rye, NY
914-798-5213
Special thanks to Connie Mintzer
and Chef Edward Leonard

LINENS:
Just Linens Ltd.
770 Lexington Avenue
New York, NY 10021
212-752-7661
justlinensltd@aol.com
Special thanks to Linda Lieberman

MONOGRAM DESIGN AND CALLIGRAPHY:
Judith Ness
1172 Park Avenue
New York, NY 10128
212-348-5863

CAKE:
Colette's Cakes
681 Washington Street
New York, NY 10014
212-366-6530
www.colettescakes.com

COUNTRY INN

LOCATION:
Willow Grove Plantation Inn
14079 Plantation Way
Orange, VA 22960
800-WG9-1778
www.willowgroveinn.com
Special thanks to Angela Mulloy
and staff

LINENS:
Just Linens Ltd.
(see page 187 for contact
information)

VINEYARD

LOCATION:
Wölffer Estate
139 Sagg Road
Sagaponack, NY 11962
631-537-5106
www.wolffer.com
Special thanks to Kim Folks and
Roman Roth

TABLES, CHAIRS, CHINA, CRYSTAL, FLATWARE:
TriServe Party Rentals
770 Lexington Avenue
New York, NY 10021
212-752-7661
www.triserpartyrental.com
Special thanks to Lance York and
Errin Verdesca

LINENS AND CHAIR COVERS:
Just Linens Ltd.
(see page 187 for contact information)

CATERING:
Janet O'Brien Caterers Inc.
Box 2306
Sag Harbor, NY 11963
631-725-9557
www.janetobriencaterers.com

CAKE:
Carlo's Bakery
95 Washington Street
Hoboken, NJ 07030
201-659-3671
www.carlosbakery.com
Special thanks to Buddy Valastro, who
also designed the cakes shown on the
jacket and half-title page.

PLACE CARDS:
Kristina Wrenn for twentyandseven
80 Chambers Street, Suite 14D
New York, NY 10007
212-566-6667
www.twentyandseven.com

BOTANIC GARDEN

LOCATION:
New York Botanical Garden
Bronx, NY 10458
718-817-8700
www.nybg.org

TABLES, CHAIRS, CHINA, CRYSTAL, FLATWARE:
TriServe Party Rentals
(see page 187 for contact information)

LINENS:
Just Linens Ltd.
(see page 187 for contact information)

CAKE:
Confetti Cakes
102 West 87th Street
New York, NY 10024
212-877-9580
www.confetticakes.com
Special thanks to Elisa Strauss

CALLIGRAPHY:
Kristina Wrenn for twentyandseven
(see above for contact information)

AT HOME

CHINA, CRYSTAL, FLATWARE:
TriServe Party Rentals
(see page 187 for contact information)

LINENS:
Just Linens Ltd.
(see page 187 for contact information)
Special thanks to Scott and Nancy for
the use of their home.

MUSEUM

LOCATION:
Chelsea Art Museum
556 West 22nd Street
New York, NY 10011
212-255-0719
www.chelseaartmuseum.org

TABLES, CHAIRS, CHINA, CRYSTAL, FLATWARE:
TriServe Party Rentals
(see page 187 for contact information)

LINENS AND CHAIR COVERS:
Just Linens Ltd.
(see page 187 for contact information)

CATERING:
Canard Inc.
503 West 43rd Street
New York, NY 10036
212-947-2480
www.canardinc.com
Special thanks to Stephen Kennard
and Diane Grinnell

CAKE:
Ron Ben-Israel Cakes
42 Greene Street
New York, NY 10013
212-625-3369
www.weddingcakes.com

STANDARD HOTEL

LOCATION:
Sheraton Meadowlands
2 Meadowlands Plaza
East Rutherford, NJ 07073
201-896-0500
Special thanks to Richard Godfrey
and staff

LIGHTING DESIGN:
Eventlights Inc.
www.eventlights.com
Special thanks to Ken Lapham and
Tim Walsh

CHAIRS, CHINA, CRYSTAL, FLATWARE:
TriServe Party Rentals
(see page 187 for contact information)

LINENS AND CHAIR COVERS:
Just Linens Ltd.
(see page 187 for contact information)

LOFT

LOCATION:
Loft Eleven
336 West 37th Street, 11th Floor
New York, NY 10018
212-871-0940
www.lofteleven.com
Special thanks to Jim Brady and staff

TABLES, CHAIRS, CHINA, CRYSTAL, FLATWARE:
TriServe Party Rentals
(see page 187 for contact information)

LINENS AND CHAIR COVERS:
Just Linens Ltd.
(see page 187 for contact information)

CATERING:
Olivier Cheng Catering & Events
495 Broadway, 2nd Floor
New York, NY 10012
212-625-3151
www.ocnyc.com
Special thanks to Olivier Cheng,
Franck Cursat and staff

CAKE:
Colette's Cakes
(see page 187 for contact information)

BEACH

TABLES, BENCHES, CHINA, CRYSTAL, FLATWARE:
TriServe Party Rentals
(see page 187 for contact information)

LINENS:
Just Linens Ltd.
(see page 187 for contact information)

CATERING:
Clamman Seafood Market Caterer
235a North Sea Road
Southampton, NY 11968
631-283-3354
www.clamman.com
Special thanks to Tim Burke, Randy
Riess, and Jean Mackenzie

WEEKEND ITINERARY CARD:
Kristina Wrenn for twentyandseven
(see page 188 for contact information)

FARM

LOCATION:
Gedney Farm
Route 57
New Marlborough, MA 01230
800-286-3139
www.gedneyfarm.com
Special thanks to Mike Smith and
Lynn Wheeler

TABLES, CHAIRS, CHINA, CRYSTAL, FLATWARE:
TriServe Party Rentals
(see page 187 for contact information)

LINENS:
Just Linens Ltd.
(see page 187 for contact information)

GUEST FAVORS:
Arbor Day Foundation
Member Services
888-448-7337
www.arborday.org

CAKE:
Confetti Cakes
(see page 188 for contact information)

TENT

TENTS:
Northeast Tent Productions
55 Poplar Street
Stamford, CT 06907
203-961-8100

www.northeasttent.com
Special thanks to Steve Bombino
and Steve Curtin

P.J. McBride Inc. Party Tent Rentals
8 Lamar Street
West Babylon, NY 11704
631-643-2848
www.pjmcbride.com

TABLES, CHAIRS, CHINA, CRYSTAL, FLATWARE:
TriServe Party Rentals
(see page 187 for contact information)

LINENS AND CHAIR COVERS:
Just Linens Ltd.
(see page 187 for contact information)

LIGHTING DESIGN:
Eventlights Inc.
www.eventlights.com

CALLIGRAPHY FOR HANGING ESCORT CARDS:
Judith Ness
(see page 187 for contact information)

GENERAL RESOURCES:

CONTAINERS, CANDLES AND FLORAL SUPPLIES:
Jamali Garden Supplies
www.jamaligarden.com
Special thanks to Biman and Juan Valerio

PAPER GOODS:
Paper Access
www.paperaccess.com

PROP RENTALS:
Chelsea Marketplace
www.chelseamarketplace.com
Special thanks to Shirley Domingo

NOTE: If you can't find what you
need in this list, visit our website
at www.karenbussen.com for
more information and links to
great resources.

index

Ambience
  beach, 153
  botanic garden, 95
  country inn, 74
  farm, 165
  home, 107
  hotel, 129
  loft, 142
  museum/gallery, 117
  private club, 65
  restaurant, 52
  tent, 178
  vineyard, 82, 85, 86
arbors, 96, 104, 111

Bar. See liquor and wines
bathrooms, 104, 108, 155, 176, 178
beach venue, 42, 46, 148–59
  reality check, 157
Ben-Israel, Ron, 120
botanic garden venue, 91–101
  reality check, 101
bouquets, 26, 78, 119, 162
  personalized, 95
  of simple flowers, 138
  simplified, 8, 22, 82
bridal party, 47, 135, 158
  gifts for, 7, 26, 89
bride's family, 30, 33, 104
bride's gown and veil, 78, 101, 157
budget, 29–39
  botanic garden costs, 97
  fixed vs. flexible, 33–34, 36, 37, 38
  funding sources, 30–32, 36
  loft plan, 144–45
  national average, 36
  negotiation, 30, 38, 77
  off-season booking, 76
  priority focus, 19, 33, 36, 37
  quantity discounts, 39, 132
  simple vs. cheap, 10, 38, 39
  simplification, 23, 25, 36, 37–39, 138

tent costs, 33, 176–77, 181
  See also splurge items
buffets, 18, 120, 123, 146, 154, 157, 181, 182

Cake, 55, 67, 69, 132
  art-inspired, 120, 123
  cupcake alternative, 98
  dessert table vs., 147
  edible flowers on, 98, 100
  geometric, 142
  groom's, 77
  individual, 68
  tea-stained, 170
  vineyard theme, 85
Canard Caterers, 120, 123
candleholders, 65, 107
candlelight, 23, 78, 128–29, 144
candle-lighting ceremony, 22, 45, 46, 50
candles, 46, 59
  centerpiece, 12, 19, 21, 65, 86, 87, 130, 157
  museum/gallery restrictions, 123
  See also specific types
Carlo's Bakery (Hoboken, N.J.), 85
caterers. See vendors
centerpieces, 8, 15, 21, 130, 141
  bud vases, 52
  clustered vases vs., 22, 25, 29, 36, 39, 182
  floating, 12, 19, 145, 157
  grapes and breadsticks, 86, 87, 88
  holiday, 74
  plants, 36, 97–98
  produce, 166, 167, 170
  quality of, 25
  seasonal, 168
  silver compote, 65
  specific flower, 98, 101, 135
  upside-down flowers, 114
  See also candles

ceremony, 41–47
  beach, 42, 46, 150, 157–58
  botanic garden, 96, 98, 101
  country inn, 72
  farm, 162, 170, 171
  hotel, 129
  museum/gallery, 123
  personalization of, 21–22, 47, 101
  private club, 62
  restaurant, 56
  simplicity of, 22, 42
  inside tent, 181
  outside tent, 176, 178
  vineyard, 82, 87, 88
chairs, 41, 104, 162
  beach venue, 153, 154
  bride's and groom's, 85
  covered, 62, 119, 135, 174
  flower-decorated, 119, 129, 177
  hotel, 129, 130, 132, 135
chambers of commerce, 18, 92
champagne fountain, 135
Chelsea Art Museum (N.Y.C.), 114
children, 110, 158
cigars, 68
citronella, 157, 179
Clam Man Caterers, 154
cleaning service, 110
clubs. See private club venue
cocktail hour, 30, 59, 88, 123, 135, 146, 153, 170
  buffet-style, 18
  tent for, 176, 177, 182, 184
Colette's Cakes, 142
colors
  beach, 153, 157, 158
  bold combinations, 15
  botanic garden, 95, 96–97, 101
  ceremony, 45–46
  country inn, 74
  for each space, 18
  farm, 165
  home, 107

hotel, 129, 130, 132, 135
  limits on, 11, 18, 65, 101
  loft, 45, 138, 142, 145
  museum/gallery, 117
  private club, 65
  restaurant, 52
  tent, 174, 178, 182, 184
  as theme, 25
  vineyard, 85, 88–89
Confetti Cakes, 170
contracts, 19, 101, 184
costs. See budget
country club. See private club venue
country inn venue, 70–79
  reality check, 77
creative thinking, 19, 29, 39
crests, 67, 68

Dance, 68, 101, 166, 171
décor, 11, 12, 21, 22, 29
  beach, 153
  botanic garden, 92
  country inn, 74, 76, 77, 78
  farm, 165, 170
  focus in, 12, 19, 21
  home, 109
  hotel, 126
  house of worship, 42, 45
  indoor ceremony, 45–46
  loft, 45, 138, 145
  museum/gallery, 117
  outdoor ceremony, 47
  private club, 66
  restaurant, 57
  tent, 178, 181, 184
  vineyard, 85
  See also colors; motifs; theme
dessert table, 147
destination weddings
  beach, 150
  country inn, 71, 78
  definition of, 15
  farm, 165, 171
  vineyard, 82